THE
POWER
OF
COMMITMENT

JERRY WHITE

T · H · E
POWER OF
COMMITMENT

DISCOVERING THE POTENTIAL OF A COMMITTED LIFE

NAVPRESS Ⓐ®

A MINISTRY OF THE NAVIGATORS

P.O. Box 6000, Colorado Springs, Colorado 80934

The Navigators is an international Christian organization. Jesus Christ gave His followers the Great Commission to go and make disciples (Matthew 28:19). The aim of The Navigators is to help fulfill that commission by multiplying laborers for Christ in every nation.

NavPress is the publishing ministry of The Navigators. NavPress publications are tools to help Christians grow. Although publications alone cannot make disciples or change lives, they can help believers learn biblical discipleship, and apply what they learn to their lives and ministries.

© 1985 by Jerry White
All rights reserved, including translation
Library of Congress Catalog Card
    Number: 85-60708
ISBN: 0-89109-178-5
11783

Cover illustration: Quang Ho

First printing, paperback edition, 1987

Printed in the United States of America

Contents

Author

Jerry White is Executive Director of The Navigators. He first came in contact with The Navigators as a student at the University of Washington. He maintained close contact throughout his military career, and helped begin Navigator ministries at the United States Air Force Academy in 1964 and at Purdue University in 1966. He was a regional director in the United States for 10 years.

Jerry's 13½ years of active service in the Air Force included duty as a mission controller at Cape Canaveral during the most active phase of the U.S. space flight program. He resigned from active duty in 1973.

He served as associate professor of astronautics at the United States Air Force Academy for six years, and co-authored a nationally recognized textbook on astrodynamics. He holds a bachelor's degree in electrical engineering from the University of Washington, a master's degree in astronautics from the Air Force Institute of Technology, and a doctorate in astronautics from Purdue University.

In addition to *The Power of Commitment,* Jerry has also written *Honesty, Morality, and Conscience, Making the Grade: A Guide to Excellence in College,* and *The Church and the Parachurch: An Uneasy Marriage.* He and his wife, Mary, are the authors of *Your Job: Survival or Satisfaction, The Christian in Mid-life,* and *Friends and Friendship.*

The White family lives in Colorado Springs, Colorado.

TO
Cecil and Thelma Davidson,
friends who have demonstrated
the life of commitment,
and who represent present and former
Navigator staff
who have laid the foundation of many
generations of committed disciples

Preface

During the past twenty-five years I have observed hundreds of Christian men and women as they have dealt with the complexities of normal living. Some flourished spiritually; others floundered. Some made an impact; others made no mark whatever. Some grew in Christ; others dried up spiritually and withered away. Some rejoiced and offered encouragement; others complained and griped. Some deepened and softened; others became more shallow and hardened. Some grew old with grace and godly influence; others just grew old.

As I observed those whose lives clearly reflected deep spiritual growth and those who seemed to stagnate, I searched for the issue that represented the fork in the road that led to their present state.

I believe the foundational issue is specific commitment—whether it was or was not made at a crucial point in life. Ordinary people who make simple, spiritual commitments under the lordship of Jesus Christ make an extraordinary impact on their world. Education, gifts, and abilities do not make the difference. Commitment does.

This issue has been burning in my heart for a number of years. The outline of this book sat in a folder for five years until I sensed the clear leading of God to write. But as I wrote, I sensed my personal inadequacy and my lack of commitment. Every word I put on paper struck at my own heart. I found I personally needed the challenge of each chapter. More than anything I have written, this represents the deepest cry of my heart.

In reading these chapters, you may be frustrated

9

that no list of pat answers is given. The book is incomplete. Its purpose is to stimulate your thinking and to drive you to your personal answers, not mine.

May God use this study to stir you to the deepest possible commitment of your mind, heart, and will.

Part One
The Basics of Commitment

1
The Uncommitted Society

BUT YOU ARE A CHOSEN RACE, A ROYAL
PRIESTHOOD, A HOLY NATION, A
PEOPLE FOR GOD'S OWN POSSESSION,
THAT YOU MAY PROCLAIM THE
EXCELLENCIES OF HIM WHO HAS
CALLED YOU OUT OF DARKNESS INTO
HIS MARVELOUS LIGHT.
1 Peter 2:9

Committed!
No turning back.
No way out.
The very thought sends chills up the spines of
so many whose lives thrive on non-commitment.
Whether in a marriage, a mortgage, or a move, they
fear that ultimate prison of never turning back.

Keep all options open. Never make a commitment to anything unless absolutely forced into it.
Ellen Goodman, a syndicated columnist, calls this
person an "option tender." This person "works carefully at his job, but always has a resume out. . . .

Others value commitment . . . he values options. . . .
His father had obligations, he has freedom; where
his father had a wife, three children, a mortgage
and a vice-presidency, he has—options." She then
wonders, "When do options become emptiness?"[1]

The fear of commitment is epidemic in the
Western world. Students wait longer and longer
to make a choice of major. Couples enter marriage
tentatively with an easy escape clause. Men and
women take jobs with a wary reserve that keeps
them looking for something better. Company
workers rarely demonstrate loyalty and commitment. Couples postpone having children to retain
their personal freedom and options. Children find
themselves in the backwash of mothers and fathers
pursuing their personal freedom.

What is the root?

Selfishness.

It is not fear or hesitancy to take a calculated
risk. It is just plain selfishness. Chuck Swindoll
calls it the "do-your-own-thing sindrome."[2] The
malady of self-centeredness permeates our affluent
Western society. So much is available and so many
opportunities are there for the grabbing. So why
not grab? If I don't, others will.

But surely Christians—evangelical Christians—
do not fall into that same trap, do we? Unfortunately,
we often do. Living in the midst of such a society,
we are caught up in a whirlpool so vast that we
hardly sense that we are being drawn into its center.
Almost unknowingly we succumb.

Among Christians, non-commitment takes on
subtle forms. Activities, church attendance, and
right doctrine can easily mask a lack of deep com-

mitment of the whole person.

Evangelical Christianity today enjoys great public acceptance and visibility. Yet the gap between the Church and secularized society grows ever wider. The majority of students entering college have virtually no knowledge of the Scriptures or the definition of a Christian—and they don't care. They have developed a totally secular mind-set.

Where is the impact of the evangelical church? Are we reaching the lost or just reorganizing the believers? Although there are success stories of Christians reaching their communities, on the whole are we not seeing an actual decline in effectiveness? If so, the problem is not that we do not have gifted and dedicated pastors and leaders. The lack is in committed lay people doing the work of the ministry. They are the ones most in touch with the world—not the pastors or Christian workers.

Many factors produce this lack of commitment. It is easy to be a Christian in our society today. It is wholly acceptable, even commendable. It takes so little in the way of commitment to be totally accepted in the world and in the church. The demands are small. Compare this to the level of commitment required in a society where Christians are despised or persecuted.

But there is more to lack of commitment than ease of living. It is a creeping worldliness, a desire to be a Christian, but to live like a non-Christian—not so much in the blatantly immoral areas, but in lifestyle. The accoutrements of wealth, position, power, and success take their silent, demanding toll on the Christian who begins to value them. The alarming increase among Christians in such things as the divorce rate and alcoholism gives but a small glimpse into the problem. The cause is much deeper, emanating from the small decisions and attitudes of years past which make today's decisions inevitable. Lack of commitment to God eventually takes its toll. We have been terribly weakened by this insidious conformity to the way of the world.

Are we no longer a "peculiar people"?[3] Must we always make the mistake of Israel in wanting a king so they could be "like all the nations"?[4] The innate desire to conform to those about us infects adults as well as adolescents. We are never immune.

We certainly do not want to return to the ultra-legalism of the past, which virtually severed communication and influence with the non-Christian. But surely there is a limit—a balance—a way of life that is God-honoring and yet builds bridges to the non-Christian.

There is another side. Many people make strong commitments to the wrong things. They knowingly commit their lives to a career, success, leisure, a lovely home, a summer cottage, an extensive wardrobe, or a time-consuming hobby. Their intensity of commitment leaves no room for more significant commitments to God. They are believers who consciously opt for lesser commitments.

But why would anyone make such an absurdly incompatible choice? Ignorance? Carnality? Sin? Yes, but for many it is simply that the cost of true Christian commitment is too high. Every commitment involves a cost. Every day a clatter of voices clamors for commitment: *Buy this. Go here. Eat ours.* All commitments cost something—money, time, energy—and some cost one's very life. The foray into the seemingly fleeting act of immorality signs a commitment that can never be fully undone. The commitment to pursue success consumes lives and families by the thousands.

Many commitments are obvious, sealed by a signature given to a bank or a company to buy a home or to join a club. "Sign on the dotted line" is the goal of a salesman, couched in terms of enjoyment and indulgence.

Other commitments are made silently as we give ourselves to a way of life or a way of thinking. Success. Financial security. Retirement. Social recognition. Materialism. They creep in and seal our commitment to them as securely as a legal document. We trap ourselves in the step-by-step decisions of days past and find ourselves so far into a system that we cannot back out.

We step over the age line of sixty and look back to find that we committed ourselves to the wrong things, and it is too late to rebuild and recommit. Certainly we can change after sixty, but all of life past seems a virtual waste.

Most Christians want to commit themselves to God. They don't want to live wasted lives.

A few years ago I was bodysurfing at a southern California beach. It was exhilarating! But as I rode one wave, I was caught in the undertow, and I found myself helpless. I was dribbled along the sandy bottom taking in water and losing breath. I was finally spit up on the beach, exhausted and very grateful.

I had desperately wanted out. But having committed myself to the thrill of riding the waves, I could not escape the eventual experience of being drawn under on one of my "rides." My choice was made long before I was really aware of the danger.

Early choices set the course of life—often small choices that seem insignificant at the time.

If Christians really understand commitment from God's viewpoint, many will respond with godly fervor. That is the purpose of this small book—to clearly describe commitment to the lordship of Christ and to help ordinary believers make significant commitments in every area of their lives.

With the great numbers of believers in evangelical churches today, the world ought to be turned upside down. But, sadly, our twentieth-century world has yet to see the impact of vast numbers of deeply committed Christians. Jonathan Edwards, an eighteenth-century theologian and preacher, clearly stated his commitment:

Resolved: To follow God with all my heart.

Resolved also: Whether others do or not, I will.

NOTES
1. Ellen Goodman, "Opting for non-commitment," *Seattle Times*, December 2, 1979, page M-1.
2. Charles R. Swindoll. *Growing Strong in the Seasons of Life* (Portland, Oregon: Multnomah Press, 1983), page 387.
3. 1 Peter 2:9, KJV
4. 1 Samuel 8:5

2
Biblical Commitment

GOD WANTS US ALL, AND HE WILL NOT
REST TILL HE GETS US ALL. NO PART
OF THE MAN WILL DO.
A. W. Tozer

As a young Christian, I was often confused by calls for commitment and dedication. What I heard was, "If you are *really* committed, you will give yourself to the full-time ministry—the pastorate or a mission field." I would sweat in the pew, reluctant to make an emotional commitment. Then I would become angry or upset, knowing that I could be committed without going to Outer Mongolia as a missionary. I wanted to commit myself to God, but could not see how to practically do it. As a trained engineer, I rejected an emotional pull.

I also knew that commitment was more than an

intellectual assent. Words like *sanctification, lordship,* and *surrender* were specific terms with vague meanings. I harbored a mixture of desire and fear—a desire to follow God fully and a fear that it would demand being full-time. Even in the midst of this confusion, I saw the need to make some clearly God-directed decisions.

As I grew in Christ, my commitment to Him clarified and deepened. Yet as a career-oriented layman, I was still confused about equating full-time service and true commitment. As I became deeply involved in the strongly lay-oriented ministry of The Navigators, the challenge to "sell the farm" or "get with it" clouded the true meaning of commitment. I sensed it was far more significant than changing vocations. Yet through The Navigators' constant drumbeat on the lordship of Christ, the meaning of commitment began to clarify.

Commitment in the Bible

Commitment is not a concise biblical doctrine such as faith, justification, grace, or sin. Rather, it is a summary word embodying several concepts of the Christian life. The word *commitment* as a noun is never used. However, the verb *commit* is used a number of times. Its primary meaning is "to entrust something to another." Some synonyms are:

to vow
to pledge
to decide
to swear
to choose
to promise

Note that these are active verbs. They are actions of commitment, each with a different shade of meaning or emphasis. We see several scriptural examples.

In seeking refuge from his enemies, David said to the Lord, "Into Thy hand I commit my spirit."[1] His safety was dependent on his God. His commitment would have been useless were not two factors present. The first was the trustworthiness of the One to whom David committed himself. The second was David's act of placing himself under God's care.

Commitment must have meaning and substance to be valid. In Psalm 37:5 David urged, "Commit your way to the Lord, trust also in Him, and He will do it." Here we see the two-way concept of commitment. We commit, and God performs in response to the commitment. His faithfulness is not dependent on our acts of commitment, but we activate His response by our commitment.

The various kinds of commitment can be categorized as follows:

1. An unconditional commitment on God's part in giving us something *(didomi)*. For an example, see Ephesians 3:7.
2. A God-initiated action to extend something to a person who must then respond in faithfulness. (*Pisteuo* is the root word for faith. In classical Greek it means a trusting, a bond by a treaty, or a contractual relation or a trust.)
3. A person entrusting something to God or to another person (*paratithemi*—in classical Greek, a commercial term meaning to commit, to deposit, to entrust).

4. A pledge or a promise to do. This can be a positive pledge, such as to perform some act. It can also be a negative pledge, such as to refrain from a particular sin or action. See Hebrews 10:23-25, 12:1-2, and 13:15,17.

In each case except the first, there is an initiator and a responder, both with required responsibilities for the contract to function. All of these commitments have biblical roots and are still valid for Christians today.

Let's examine each of these briefly.

God unconditionally commits. God is the Great Initiator of the eternal commitment—with Moses, with Abraham, with David, and finally, with Christ in the New Covenant. In each, He sovereignly instituted His commitment to His people. To Abraham He said, "I will make you a great nation, and I will bless you."[3] The great "I will" from the One who declared Himself as the great "I AM" reverberates through history as God relentlessly initiates His commitment to mankind.

In Christ, God embodied the fulfillment of His eternal covenant and "has given [committed] all judgment to the Son."[4] The same word is used in 1 Corinthians 1:4, referring to the giving of grace in Christ, and in 2 Corinthians 1:22, referring to the Holy Spirit: God "sealed us and gave [*didomi*] us the Spirit in our hearts as a pledge." Here we see God's sovereign giving resulting in a pledge or commitment to us.

In Galatians 1:4 we read that Jesus "gave Himself for our sins." This was His sovereign, irrevocable commitment to the cross for our justification. In Ephesians 3:7, Paul acknowledges the sovereign source of his ministry to the Gentiles: "I was made a minister [passive voice, God's action], according to the gift of God's grace which was given to me [*didomi*] according to the working of His power."

This is but a sampling of the ways in which God commits Himself to the believer.

God entrusts, man responds. The Greek word *pisteuo* is the root word for faith. In this context, the teaching is that of faith in Christ for salvation, believing in Him to receive life eternal. In this sense, we entrust ourselves to God for our salvation.

But God also entrusts something to men that requires their obedience and response. Paul says that he was "entrusted with the gospel to the uncircumcised."[5] He then went to the uncircumcised. In 1 Thessalonians 2:4 we read that Paul, Silvanus, and Timothy were "approved by God to be entrusted with the gospel, *so we speak.*"

God commits and man responds. A trust is given. A trust is kept. In classical Greek one meaning was "one who is bound by an oath, contract, pledge, etc., and who may then be relied on."[6] This two-way commitment penetrates much of our Christian lives in the areas of marriage, money, abilities, and responsibilities. God commits something to us, and we commit its use to God.

Man entrusts, God responds. A third commitment is initiated by man, and God or another person responds. *Paratithemi* was once used as a commercial term signifying a deposit or a trust, much as we deposit a sum of money in a bank for safekeeping.

Timothy was instructed to commit the teaching

he received from Paul to faithful men for safe-keeping.[7] Christians are instructed to "entrust their souls to a faithful Creator" as they encounter suffering.[8]

In many issues of our lives we commit something to God, and He responds to that trust. Similarly we commit things to other people, and they respond to that trust. This basic idea of commitment has a multitude of practical applications that following chapters will address.

Man vows, God enables. The last form of commitment involves clear decisions to do or not to do something. For instance, Paul "determined to know nothing . . . except Jesus Christ, and Him crucified."[9] He made a decision on how he would conduct himself. According to 1 Corinthians 9:25-27, Paul also decided to exercise self-control as he lived his life.

Throughout Scripture we find men and women coming to decisions about what they will or will not do. And in each case, the person decides, but God enables him to carry out that decision. God is the One who strengthens us as we follow through on the decisions we make: "The God of all grace, who called you to His eternal glory in Christ, will Himself perfect, confirm, strengthen and establish you."[10] Choices are made daily, and God enables daily.

So we see three fundamental types of commitment in which man has an option to act:

1. A commitment to accept the responsibility of something that God entrusts to his care.
2. A commitment to entrust something to God dependent upon His faithfulness to fulfill the trust.

3. A commitment or pledge to do or not do some particular act.

These three commitments will intertwine themselves inseparably throughout each of the practical life applications in this book.

The Focus of Commitment

To this point, theory and theology have formed the basis of consideration. Now reality must set in. How does a believer activate commitment in his life? Is it just an unexplainable mystical experience? Or can we bring it to bear in the nitty-gritty of real life?

True commitment focuses on three essential parts of a person's life—the *mind, heart,* and *will.* In this discussion I will use these words to describe the intellectual, emotional, and volitional aspects of a person's life.[11] Commitment must involve all three to be valid. The lack of any one over a long period results in the collapse of commitment. The three may not become involved at once, nor is there a fixed sequence. Yet the ultimate goal is to unite all of them in true commitment.

The *mind* grapples with knowledge. It takes in the knowledge of God from the Scriptures and begins to absorb its meaning. It sifts truth and tests its validity. The mind wrestles with words and meanings—and makes a judgment. When Jesus repeated the great commandment to "love the Lord your God with all your heart, and with all your soul, and with all your *mind*,"[12] He counted the mind as a necessary part of the commitment process.

The mind can be focused: "Set your mind on

the things above."[13] The mind is to be "fully con-
vinced," or persuaded.[14] The mind decides not to
do specific acts that may cause others to stumble,[15]
and thus interacts with the will. God revealed to
Job that He gave understanding to the mind of
man.[16] Nehemiah pondered in his mind some charges
brought against some Jews in Jerusalem and then
acted to take issue with the corrupt elders.[17]

Yet the mind is not infallible. It can be deceived
by a focus on sin and the flesh, and become insensitive or confused. It must be activated by a focus
on the Spirit of God.[18] The mind simply processes
the information that it is fed. Thus it must be fed
the truth of Scripture to make godly judgments.

When the mind is confronted with the need for
true spiritual commitment, it sifts the words of
Scripture and the preaching of godly men and comes
to an understanding of the decisions that must be
made. But knowing and understanding the truth
fall far short of a life of consistent commitment.

Judas knew what was wrong, but he still
betrayed Christ. David clearly knew the wrong of
his sin with Bathsheba, but he still pursued that
heartbreaking chain of events. Saul knew he should
not presumptuously take holy sacrifices into his
own hands, but he did. Christian men and women
know they should not commit adultery, but they
decide to do it anyway. Christians know they ought
to obey God, but they choose not to.

Knowledge begins the process of true spiritual
commitment, but it needs the extension to heart
and will. Peter expressed it well when he said, "Gird
your minds for action."[19] The set of mind must
lead to godly action.

Heart refers to that aspect of the person that embraces emotionally the reality of that which the mind analyzed. We emphasize emotions when we speak of the heart in this writing. The biblical usage of the word *heart* is quite complex and is certainly beyond the narrow concept of emotions. Yet I plead tolerance in using it more narrowly for the emotive part of a human being, with the understanding that it is clearly interdependent, especially with the mind. The two together more closely resemble the whole person.[20]

The Scriptures teach us that the heart loves, it rejoices in the Lord, it grieves, and it desires.[21] Yet it is not distinguished completely from mind and will. It performs intellectual functions: it discerns right from wrong, it disbelieves, and it instructs the mind.[22] It also performs volitional or will functions: it turns us to God, and it trusts in God.[23] Some of its functions, like joy, are clearly emotional, while others, like courage and thankfulness, might have as much to do with intellect and will as with emotions.[24]

The heart, like the mind, is not infallible: it lusts, it can be hardened, it hates, it despises, it groans, it becomes angry, it cherishes sin, it becomes proud, it rejects correction, and it plots evil.[25]

"Trust in the Lord with all your heart,"[26] not just with all your mind. The mind cannot trust of itself. Trust is the prerogative of the heart in concert with the mind. The mind and heart must function together. David said, "Examine me, O Lord, and try me; *test my mind and my heart*."[27] David was a man of the heart. His son Solomon was a man of the mind. David sinned, and his heart smote him.

Solomon sinned, and his mind excused him. David wept. Solomon lusted.

When the heart acts without truth in the mind, it becomes deceived. Emotional responses alone can never sustain commitment. Heart commitment goes far beyond emotion. It must tap the deepest wells of one's inner being. God cannot be put in a box. He sometimes will break through the thick crust of our being at a solely emotional level and drive us to commitment. But it will not last without the significant infusion of scriptural truth to the mind.

David's *mind* knew what was right. After his sin, his *heart* led him to repentance. Yet he failed to exercise his *will* to do what was right in the matter of Bathsheba and her husband, Uriah. His place and his position blinded his heart and mind, allowing him to willfully disobey God. The final link to true commitment is the exercise of the will—decision.

Paul instructed slaves in Ephesus to be obedient, "doing the will of God from the heart."[28] Obedience must flow from the heart. But most importantly, obedience must flow. All the right thinking in the mind and right feeling in the heart can never justify the failure to *do* what is right. "Therefore, to one who knows the right thing to do, and does not do it, to him it is sin."[29]

Sin.

Not just an error. Or an oversight. But sin.

James invariably marries faith (based on knowledge and heart belief) with obedience—not as a condition for salvation, but as a requisite for a committed life. Then obedience is finally an act of the will. One well-known, godly man was asked how he managed to get up in the morning to spend time with

God. "Well," he said, "I put one leg over the edge of the bed, then the other." Simple. An act of the will, not a rush of longing desire.

Mind. Heart. Will. These aspects of the whole person are inseparable and essential for Christ-centered, biblical commitment.

The mind is the seat of intellect and knowledge, resulting in theology.

The heart is the seat of belief and affection, resulting in a desire for God.

The will is the seat of decision and obedience, resulting in a holy life.

What happens when some are missing?

Mind only leads to an intellectual theology devoid of real life.

Heart only leads to unstable emotionalism without true biblical basis and without the life of obedience to accompany it.

Will only leads to legalism without the knowledge of the Word and without depth in the life.

Mind and heart only lead to commitment that never gets applied to the real issues of life.

Mind and will only lack the joy of relationship and loving service to God.

Heart and will only lead to aberration of commitment without a biblical basis.

We need the Word of God to nurture us in truth, the Spirit of God to guide our affections, and the lordship of Christ to teach us loving obedience.

Summary

True biblical commitment expresses itself much like a contract between God and man. One initiates.

The other responds. Whether we initiate or respond, the key party to the contract is God Himself. It is His trustworthiness that validates any action on our part. He is faithful and He is sovereign. He is not our puppet in "making deals" in commitment, yet He responds according to His Word and His promises as we make thoughtful, loving, and obedient commitments. Each commitment bears the necessary human steps of mind, heart, and will. And each bears the sovereign work of a loving God as He takes each faltering commitment and molds it—and us—into His image in the process.

We must act. We cannot sit back passively and hope for holiness. It comes only with deliberate commitments made through the years in the midst of life.

A.W. Tozer, the powerful Christian writer of the past few decades, wrote concerning the commitment to exalt God in our lives:

> In speaking thus I have one fear; it is that I may convince the mind before God can win the heart. For this God-above-all position is one not easy to take. The mind may approve it while not having the consent of the will to put it into effect.
> While the imagination goes ahead to honor God, the will may lag behind and the man never knows how divided his heart is. The whole man must make the decision before the heart can know any satisfaction.[30]

NOTES
1. Psalm 31:5
2. Gerhard Kittell, *Theological Dictionary of the New*

Testament (Grand Rapids, Michigan: Wm. B. Eerdmans Publishing Co., 1964), 6:175.
3. Genesis 12:2
4. John 5:22
5. Galatians 2:7
6. Kittell, 6:178
7. 2 Timothy 2:2
8. 1 Peter 4:19
9. 1 Corinthians 2:2
10. 1 Peter 5:10
11. In this discussion I do not intend to address the question of whether man is dichotomous (body and soul) or trichotomous (body, soul, and spirit). Mind, heart, and will are certainly intricately integrated in the exquisite creation of mankind. Yet we can see the three in action practically and we see them used individually in Scripture.
12. Matthew 22:37
13. Colossians 3:2
14. Romans 14:5
15. Romans 14:13, NIV
16. Job 38:36
17. Nehemiah 5:7, NIV
18. Romans 8:6-7
19. 1 Peter 1:13
20. In the Old Testament, the Hebrew word is *leb*, or *lebab*. It is used in a physical or figurative sense 29 times, for the personality, inner life, or character 257 times, for emotional states or consciousness 166 times, for intellectual activities 204 times, and for volition and purpose 195 times (J.D. Douglas, editor, *The New Bible Dictionary* [Wm. B. Eerdmans Publishing Co., 1962], page 509). Its predominant usage is in reference to the whole person, yet it does speak of varied aspects of that person.
      Such is also the case in the New Testament word *kardia*. W.E. Vine states that "the word came to stand for man's entire mental and moral activity, both the rational and the emotional elements" (W.E. Vine, *Dictionary of New Testament Words*, Vol. II [Old Tappan, New Jersey: Fleming H. Revell, 1940], page 206).
      The word *psyche* denotes a person's entire soul-life.
21. Deuteronomy 6:5, 1 Samuel 2:1, 1 Samuel 2:33, 2 Samuel 3:21
22. 1 Kings 3:9, Proverbs 14:1, Psalm 16:7
23. Psalm 27:8, Psalm 28:7

24. Psalm 28:7, Galatians 4:8, Colossians 3:16
25. Proverbs 6:25, Exodus 7, Leviticus 19:17, 2 Samuel
    6:16, Psalm 38:8, Psalm 39:3, Psalm 66:18, NIV,
    Psalm 101:5, Proverbs 5:12, Proverbs 8:19
26. Proverbs 3:5
27. Psalm 26:2
28. Ephesians 6:6
29. James 4:17
30. A.W. Tozer, *The Pursuit of God* (Harrisburg,
    Pennsylvania: Christian Publications, Inc., 1968),
    page 107.

3
Commitment and Lordship

AND WHY DO YOU CALL ME,
"LORD, LORD," AND DO NOT DO
WHAT I SAY?
Luke 6:46

It is an electric moment. God has clearly spoken to hearts as I have talked about the lordship of Christ. The audience, person by person, focuses on what God is saying to them. As I close in prayer, I comment, "I know God is speaking to some of you clearly about lordship issues in your life. In fact, I'm sure many of you have privately made specific lordship commitments already tonight. I have found that it is often helpful to express those commitments publicly. For some of you, this is the first time you have ever made a full commitment to the lordship of Christ in your life. If you have made a significant personal commitment, would you simply stand where you are to make this public as I pray for your decision." Almost immediately, dozens stand. I simply pray for them and close the meeting—without fanfare, emotion, or further public display.

Afterwards, over coffee, a conversation takes place.

"I appreciate what Jerry shared tonight, but I have some problems with his application."

"How is that?" asks his companion.

"He implied that a person can ask Christ to be his Savior without being Lord, and that lordship follows at some later time. I believe that both must occur at once. You can't have cheap grace. Christ is both Lord *and* Savior—or He is neither."

His friend pauses for a few moments and then replies, "Yes, I see your point. And it is a good one. I know this is an ongoing theological debate. Even though I'm halfway through seminary now and have argued this issue from both sides, I still can't fully grasp the truth. In fact, I'm a bit confused."

"What is it that confuses you?"

"Frankly, it's part of my own experience. A few years ago, I stood up for a similar commitment. It was the turning point of my Christian life. I clearly knew I was a believer—no question of my salvation. Yet I also knew there were areas of my life that I had not surrendered to God. I made what I see as a total lordship commitment that evening and my life has never been the same."

"Maybe you really were born again at that point."

"No, I knew beyond a shadow of a doubt that

I had received eternal life at least two years earlier.
I wasn't rebellious or living in sin. I just knew I
had some more decisions to make."

Does this sound familiar? I have frequently
given invitations like the one I described above. And
I regularly have people tell me that such an invita-
tion brought about a turning point in their lives.
The preceding conversation is a composite of dis-
cussions about the validity of such a commitment.

Whether we call it consecration, surrender,
commitment, repentance, or revival, I see that
subsequent—and sometimes frequent—decisions
beyond salvation are biblical and necessary. Daily
obedience is never automatic. It is a conscious
decision—in fact, a decision of lordship: "Why do
you call me, 'Lord, Lord,' and do not do what I
say?"[1] Some of these subsequent decisions are far
from minor. They are life-changing. Don't misunderstand: I am not referring to a mystical second
work of grace. The Holy Spirit certainly is involved—
prompting, reminding, bringing Scripture to mind,
and pointing us to Christ.

The apostle Peter struggled with this growth
process. He had to make several significant, life-
changing decisions—all the while being under the
lordship of the pre-crucified Christ. Even after
Pentecost, Peter had to be confronted by Paul with
his hypocrisy. Some struggle more than others with
lordship and commitment.

Lordship and commitment are intimately related. Most spiritual commitments involve some
aspect of the lordship of Christ. To clarify the
meaning of commitment, we must first clarify the

meaning of lordship. Three facts stand out:

Jesus Christ is Lord.

We acknowledge Jesus Christ as Lord.

We commit ourselves to his lordship.

Jesus is Lord. He is the *Kurios*—the Owner and Master of all creation. He is Lord of the Sabbath, Lord of glory, Sovereign Lord, Lord of lords, and Lord God Almighty. Our belief or lack of belief can never change the immutable fact of His lordship. The New Testament repeatedly affirms Jesus Christ as Lord.

We acknowledge Jesus Christ as Lord. Our acknowledgment does not make Him more or less Lord. We admit it as fact—a recognition of what is. Ultimately everyone will acknowledge Jesus as Lord—willingly or unwillingly: "At the name of Jesus every knee should bow, of those who are in heaven, and on earth, and under the earth, and that every tongue should confess that Jesus Christ is Lord, to the glory of God the Father."[2] The believer willingly acknowledges Christ as Lord now. The unbeliever unwillingly does so when it is too late.

What then is the acknowledgment of the believer? "If you confess with your mouth Jesus as Lord, and believe in your heart that God raised Him from the dead, you shall be saved; for with the heart man believes, resulting in righteousness, and with the mouth he confesses, resulting in salvation."[3] Here the personal confession and the heart belief are joined to give eternal life. The belief includes acknowledging the lordship and deity of Christ as well as His sacrificial death for our sins and His ultimate victory in resurrection.

We acknowledge Christ's lordship in salvation,

but we may well not have included the total willful yielding of all areas of our life. We must abandon hope outside of Christ and give heart assent to His ownership and lordship in our life.

Jesus is Lord. Jesus is now *my* Lord. He is Owner and Master. Yet He still must exert the control over my life. Were it not so, no concepts of spiritual growth and daily conformity to His image would or could exist. Perfection would be immediate.

Thus, we are urged, "Do not be conformed to this world, but be transformed by the renewing of your mind, that you may prove what the will of God is, that which is good and acceptable and perfect."[4] The many commands of Scripture presume that one may or may not obey and respond to the lordship of Christ. One of the great mysteries of God is that as believers, we exist under the acknowledged lordship of Christ, yet we must yield to our Sovereign Lord at the many intersections of life.

Finally, *we commit ourselves to the lordship of Jesus Christ.* This is a continuing act of the mind, will, and heart—a task never quite finished. Paul's concern was to run the race with care and discipline, "lest possibly, after I have preached to others, I myself should be disqualified."[5]

The battle of mind and will that is referred to in Proverbs 7:25 rages in each believer. There is no discharge from this war. Except for the indwelling and comforting of the Holy Spirit, victory would elude us all.

This ongoing commitment occupies the focus of this book. For some unexplainable reason, redeemed men and women under the lordship of a loving Savior still struggle with commitment to that Sovereign Lord. A fog of worldliness seems to envelop them to detract, blind, and deter them from the unsurpassed joy and fulfillment that await the man and woman of commitment.

NOTES
1. Luke 6:46
2. Philippians 2:10-11
3. Romans 10:9-10
4. Romans 12:2
5. 1 Corinthians 9:27

4
Commitment, Conversion, and Emotion

BUT THE ONE WHO HAS HEARD, AND
HAS NOT ACTED ACCORDINGLY, IS LIKE
A MAN WHO BUILT A HOUSE UPON THE
GROUND WITHOUT ANY FOUNDATION;
AND THE RIVER BURST AGAINST IT AND
IMMEDIATELY IT COLLAPSED, AND
THE RUIN OF THAT HOUSE WAS GREAT.
Luke 6:49

We live in a sensual world; we face no bigger trap
than religious sensuality. If we have an ecstatic
experience with Christ we are tempted to feel he
is in the ecstatic experience rather than that he is
in all our experiences. He is in your ordinary
routine just as he is in your mystical ecstasies:
he is the down-to-earth God. Do not wait for goose
bumps to reassure you that God is near. Thank
him that he is near regardless of how you feel.
Goose bumps are acceptable if you get them, but
they really don't matter; life cannot continue a
24-hour-a-day-7-day-a-week-52-week-a-year-on-

> and-on-forever-goose-bump. It would deny your
> humanity. You are flesh, not glass. . . . Mystical
> sensations can be either of the Holy Spirit or of
> human nature, either of God or of Satan. Lots of
> Christians get mixed up worshiping their
> experiences: the idol of Christ plus their religious
> experiences. Thank God he is with you when the
> goose bumps go. Beware of spiritual lust. You are
> learning to live by raw faith.[1]

Emotions are never an accurate barometer of spiritual depth or commitment. They depend too much on our circumstances. Yet emotions are an integral part of the real person. They cannot be denied, nor can they be depended upon. Commitment is not an emotion, but emotions certainly can accompany commitment. God speaks to the heart as well as to the mind.

Religious emotion has always been a puzzle in the Christian world. None of us likes the carefully staged meeting where the singing, the dress, and the stories are all choreographed to build to an emotional pitch that leads to a "decision." Nor do we approve of the cold, mechanical formality of a service in which a robot could participate. Where is the balance? Nowhere: It is not an issue of balance, but of how God speaks to us. It is not so much the external parade of emotion as the internal sensitivity to God. Organized emotion, or lack thereof, is not the issue.

God captures our attention in two general ways: through the mind and through the emotions. One person absorbs Scripture and biblical truth, and comes to a decision before God. Another is struck emotionally and cries out to God for help. Neither is sufficient by itself. Both must lead to a decision of the will and ultimately to a combination of mind, heart, and will.

A friend of mine, Geoff Gorsuch, was an Air Force pilot in Vietnam. He presented Jesus Christ's offer of salvation to a number of his friends as they daily risked their lives in combat. Some never came back. Geoff's roommate saw the need for salvation, but simply would not make a decision. But he asked Geoff for a prayer to pray in case he got in trouble. He memorized that prayer.

A few days later he was flying on a mission. Suddenly a flame shot up from the ground and a surface-to-air missile struck his aircraft. His plane shook and began to spiral out of the sky. In desperation, he prayed his memorized prayer. Then, inexplicably, his plane righted itself and he wobbled back to an emergency base—as a new Christian!

A foxhole conversion? Certainly. God is no respecter of circumstances. The "Hound of Heaven" pursues men in every fashion—through both emotion and intellect. But there is much that must follow any conversion commitment to cause a person to grow.

Similarly, the person of rational intellect who makes decisions on the basis of fact and truth may need to be broken by God to bridge the gap of heart and mind.

In the early years of my Christian life, I rarely expressed any emotion. But as I have walked with God for a number of years, I now find that tears come frequently as God speaks to my heart. Tears in themselves mean little, but the cry of the heart to God means much to Him. Conversion to Christ can involve deep emotions, but in no way do emotions make the conversion any more valid than when one quietly prays and receives Christ.

In later commitments, emotions may or may not be present as well. As God deals with us deeply, we respond in different ways. Jeremiah was called the "weeping prophet," because he wept for his people's sins. David was an emotional man—he sang songs of the shepherd, he danced wildly in the streets after victory, he wept in the night. God uses depression, loneliness, sorrow, and fear, as well as joy, laughter, and success to get our attention. The rational Paul prayed for people with "anguish of heart" and "many tears."[2]

So the emotions are not wrong—nor are they necessary.

But aren't some commitments just emotions with no substance? Yes: The Church is filled with people who make verbal or emotional commitments and never do anything about them. They respond quickly in an emotional rush and forget them almost as quickly. Such is a mockery of true spiritual decisions. Like seed sown in shallow soil, emotional commitments quickly sprout but are just as quickly withered by the sun. They have no roots or depth.[3] An emotional commitment without the knowledge of the Word and the will to obey is no more meaningful than a pauper signing a contract for a million-dollar house. It is like a house built on sand.[4] No foundation. No roots.

The reality of commitment is not found in the warm, cozy feeling of sharing in a circle, holding hands, and singing, "We are one in the Spirit." Reality is found in being obedient in the daily grind of living, in the restless battle against sin, and in the relentless pressures of the world. And in that context, deep emotions may be trusted.

May God deliver us from rootless emotions. May He also deliver us from cold, emotionless commitments.

NOTES
1. Howard Butt, *The Velvet Covered Brick* (San Francisco: Harper & Row, 1973), page 108.
2. 2 Corinthians 2:4
3. Matthew 13:1-23
4. Luke 6:49

5
The Cost of Commitment

AND HE WAS SAYING TO THEM ALL,
"IF ANYONE WISHES TO COME
AFTER ME, LET HIM DENY HIMSELF,
AND TAKE UP HIS CROSS DAILY,
AND FOLLOW ME."
Luke 9:23

"SO THEREFORE, NO ONE OF YOU CAN
BE MY DISCIPLE WHO DOES NOT GIVE
UP ALL HIS OWN POSSESSIONS."
Luke 14:33

Preposterous! What was the man saying? He talked in riddles. Didn't Jesus know that the Messiah would restore the kingdom? What did He mean when He said "deny" and "give up"?

The disciples knew. They had seen that look in Jesus' eyes before. He was absolutely serious. Following Him would be costly. They would be mocked, hunted, beaten. It turned out that all but John died as martyrs.

What a contrast to Western Christianity today. Christianity is totally acceptable, even in vogue. Position, wealth, and power are commonplace—a four-bedroom house, two cars, a boat, and every conceivable convenience; padded pews, sound systems, and choreographed music, accompanied of course by a respectable level of giving. To the outside observer, there is virtually no difference between a Christian and his non-Christian neighbor. A happier marriage? Perhaps. A more moral life? Hopefully so. Different goals? I wonder. Christians have never worn the clothes of affluence well. Corruption often follows wealth.

Where is that first-century fervor—and persecution? Many Christians in other parts of the world face it daily, and it builds something into their character that Western Christians are losing. Many Christians face immense cost because of their identification with Christ—lost jobs, broken family ties, and poverty. For Christians in the West, there is so little obvious cost.

According to Vance Havner, "As long as the church wore scars, they made headway. When they began to wear medals, the cause languished. It was a greater day for the church when Christians were fed to the lions than when they bought season tickets and sat in the grandstand."[1] Is this really true? Or was the cost just so obvious? Perhaps then, as today, there were many who knew the cost of commitment and simply hid. In that day one became a "secret" disciple. Today public identification is easy, with little or no cost.

The Scriptures have not changed. The requisites for commitment are the same. But few are willing to count the cost.

The key is commitment—not just the big commitments, but the many smaller ones. Please do not

be deceived. Each commitment will exact a price.
The counter to commitment is sales resistance.
We are well schooled in it. We are bombarded daily
with advertisements and salespeople bent on selling
us something. But until we sign on the dotted line
or hand over the money, there is no sale. To that
point, it is all talk. And talk is cheap. So we talk
and work at avoiding the commitment. The resistance to commit to anything is ingrained in us.

This resistance carries over into our Christian
lives—and we resist commitment to the One who
owns us.

Daniel knew the meaning of commitment.
When he and his three teenage friends were carried
away captive to Babylon, he knew trying times
would come. He "made up his mind that he would
not defile himself."[2] And he didn't. He took a risk—
made his stand—and God blessed him and his
friends. They were sharp young men who excelled
in their training. Soon Daniel found himself on the
top of the heap—if being second to the king can be
called that. Jealousy and rage flew about the palace.

The king made a stupid decree that all people
could pray only to him. The palace plotters knew
well Daniel's practice of praying to God three times
daily in full view of anyone who wanted to look.
With full knowledge of the consequences—being
thrown to the lions—Daniel kept his commitment
to God. He didn't hide. He didn't scratch his brow
thoughtfully as he pretended to work on other
things. He knelt and prayed. And the plotters
caught him.

Daniel had no promise of deliverance. He
counted the cost and kept his commitment. He was

thrown to the lions. Of course you know that the lions kept him warm through the night and waited for a morning breakfast of palace plotters. But Daniel didn't know that would happen. In fact, in an earlier event, as his three friends were tossed into a furnace for their commitment, they said, "Our God whom we serve is able to deliver us from the furnace of blazing fire . . . *but even if He does not,* let it be known to you, O king, that we are not going to serve your gods."[3] The choice belonged to God. Daniel and his friends simply obeyed. Hebrews 11:32-40 records a list of events that went *both* ways for committed believers—some to victory and some to suffering and death.

Christian commitment is not like a financial investment in which you pay now for assumed return later. There is no guarantee of worldly success to pay off your sacrifice. It is true that Jesus said to his disciples, "No one who has left home or wife or brothers or parents or children for the sake of the kingdom of God will fail to receive many times as much in this age and, in the age to come, eternal life."[4] God promises to bless our obedience, but not with "two dollars given to invest—three returned in ninety days." We make the commitment and leave the results to God. In a sense, it is like signing a blank check and allowing God to fill in the amount. It can be a frightening venture. But God will never demand more from us than we have to give.

I know that when I buy something, I get only what I pay for. But I wonder if I will ever learn my lesson. It may be my home background of having very little money that causes me to constantly look for "good deals." I can't resist the sale

pages of a newspaper. I have bought more junk that
lies unused and useless.

On the other hand, I have made some good
decisions. Most of our furniture is twenty-two
years-old-hodgepodge heirloom, dating from a fire
that destroyed all our belongings. I remember
buying our dining room table. The hefty salesman
opened it up where extra leaves would be inserted
and bounced up and down on the rails to demonstrate its sturdiness. He was right. It was excellent
quality. It won't wear out. It still bears the marks
made during the meals that fed our family and
many guests. It remains as sturdy as ever, even
with the chips and dents imbedded by four children.
The higher cost was worth it.

In terms of spiritual commitments, the same
principle applies. There are no "bargain buys." The
quality of the commitment is reflected in its cost.
There are no shortcuts.

Jesus pictures the cost of discipleship in Luke
14:25-35:

> Now great multitudes were going along with Him;
> and He turned and said to them, "If anyone comes
> to Me, and does not hate his own father and mother
> and wife and children and brothers and sisters,
> yes, and even his own life, he cannot be My disciple.
> Whoever does not carry his own cross and come
> after Me cannot be My disciple. For which one of
> you, when he wants to build a tower, does not first
> sit down and calculate the cost, to see if he has
> enough to complete it? Otherwise, when he has
> laid a foundation, and is not able to finish, all
> who observe it begin to ridicule him, saying, 'This

man began to build and was not able to finish.'
Or what king, when he sets out to meet another
king in battle, will not first sit down and take
counsel whether he is strong enough with ten
thousand men to encounter the one coming against
him with twenty thousand? Or else, while the
other is still far away, he sends a delegation
and asks terms of peace. So therefore, no one of
you can be My disciple who does not give up all
his own possessions. Therefore, salt is good; but if
even salt has become tasteless, with what will
it be seasoned? It is useless either for the soil or
for the manure pile; it is thrown out. He who has
ears to hear, let him hear."

People were "going along with him." The
crowds followed Jesus willingly until the demands
of discipleship became clear. Talk of hating family
and bearing a cross were strong words. When Jesus
gave the examples of building a tower and of a king
going to war, He taught them to count the cost and
finish the job. He did not ask for blind commitment,
but careful, intelligent discipleship—fully aware of
the cost.

Jesus suddenly confronted the people with
giving up their possessions to be His disciples. It
was no idle threat. Most who followed Him had to
do just that. He spoke of salt becoming tasteless
(verse 34). It remains salt but has lost any value
for its intended use. The tasteless salt refers to
Christians who have not paid the cost of commitment. They have settled for an anemic, self-serving
form of Christian living that bears no witness to
the world around them. They are ridiculed by those

around them and don't even know it. They make only safe commitments. Their public devotion is without risk. They have embarked on a spiritual battle completely unprepared for the enemy.

No building is built in a day. No war is won just in a moment of battle. Those costly, life-changing commitments flow from a life of smaller commitments, all with some cost.

But precisely what is the cost of commitment? Time, money, promotion, reputation, energy, emotional stamina, or health—all could be part of the cost. God deals with us individually. What is to one person a great price may be a pittance to another.

The cost is great. But so is the reward—namely, the true joy of the Christian life when we hear the words, "Well done, good and faithful slave; you were faithful with a few things, I will put you in charge of many things, *enter into the joy of your master.*"[5]

There is no greater fable in the Christian life than the promise of commitment without a cost. The key to a joyful, victorious Christian life is costly commitment.

NOTES
1. J. Oswald Sanders, *Spiritual Maturity* (Chicago: Moody Press, 1962), page 110.
2. Daniel 1:8
3. Daniel 3:17-18, italics mine
4. Luke 18:29-30, NIV
5. Matthew 25:21, italics mine

Part Two
Commitment in Your Personal Life

6
Commitment in Your Spiritual Walk

AND I, BRETHREN, COULD NOT SPEAK TO
YOU AS TO SPIRITUAL MEN, BUT AS TO
MEN OF FLESH, AS TO BABES IN CHRIST.
1 Corinthians 3:1

No one is so empty as the man who has stopped walking with God and doesn't know it. He smiles at church, serves on boards, even teaches the Bible, but he is an empty spiritual shell. He lives on past knowledge and correct doctrine. He says and does the right things. But there is a hollow ring to his life. No one really notices, however, because there are so many other hollow rings around him.

He has spiritual anorexia nervosa, and he is ignorant of the disease. In the physical realm, anorexia nervosa is a disease affecting mainly women who in effect starve themselves as they compulsively diet. But the body has an irrevocable law. It must have food to live.

Spiritual anorexia is the absence of spiritual food for the spiritual body.

I once made a decision to rid myself of that middle-aged roll of fat around my waist. I skipped breakfast and lunch on a Monday, and felt fine. Tuesday I repeated the same routine. At 4 P.M. I went to play handball. I thought I would die! I had no energy. I got dizzy. I was winded. My body gave out warning signals until it got my attention.

My spiritual body doesn't force the same attention on me. I can be starving, yet almost unaware. Yes, I know I am a bit "down" on my spiritual intake, but after all, I have twenty years of reserve to draw upon. Hardly! Like the physical body, nutrition *must* come regularly or I pay the spiritual penalty.

Food, fancy or plain, is what the body needs. The basics of a healthy life are food, water, air, and exercise. There are no substitutes.

Chuck Swindoll once related a comment by the famed football coach Vince Lombardi on the basics of football: "Gentlemen, this is a football." Chuck suggested that our spiritual "coaches" need to say, "Ladies and gentlemen, this is a Bible."

The Bible—there is no substitute. It is basic, indispensable to spiritual growth. But it does not enter our spiritual beings by osmosis. It cannot help us if we place it on a shelf or tuck it under our arm. "Like newborn babes, long for the pure milk of the word, that by it you may grow."[1] Without the regular intake of the Word, *you will not grow.*

Certainly exercise, or application of Scripture,

and the illumination of the Holy Spirit must also accompany the Word, but they cannot work without the Word first infusing our lives.

Taking the Scriptures into your life is not a weekly gorging on Sunday; it is not a course in a seminary; it is not poring for hours over a passage, as good as that may be. Rather, it is the regular reading of the Word and allowing God to speak to us through it. The frequency of feeding on the Word is more important than the length of the reading.

This regular time with God takes commitment.

In 1962, when I entered graduate school, I made a clear commitment that proved to be a turning point in my life. I knew the demands that would be placed on me, and I knew my tendency to be a workaholic. Before God, I made a commitment to *daily* spend time reading the Scriptures and praying *before* I did anything else at my own option. If I got up late, I would go to class, but not study until I spent time with God. It was a clear act of the *will*. I knew missing a day of devotions or quiet time would not sink me spiritually, but I also knew I needed that decision and commitment to make me last in the long term.

Some friends of mine practice a "no Bible, no breakfast" discipline. Some read at night. Some spend time with God at other opportune times during the day. But I know of *no one* who has a deep spiritual walk who does not spend time daily with God in His Word. It is indispensable. It requires a specific commitment.

If you have never consistently practiced the spiritual discipline of a quiet time, let me share a few suggestions.

First, keep it simple. Select a book of the Bible to read through (Mark, John, Acts, Psalms, Proverbs, for example). As you read, ask God to show you what you need for your own life. Read slowly and reflect on what the Bible says. Pray about it. Then write a few lines in a notebook on what God spoke to you about. This can take from five to thirty minutes, depending on how much time you plan to spend. Then pray for yourself, others, your day, key events, and your witness.[2]

But why do this? Just to be disciplined? No. The focus must be the presence of Jesus Christ. We want a loving relationship with the living Christ. He must take preeminence in our lives. The quiet time is for fellowship with Christ, not just absorption of the Bible. Scripture helps us know the mind of Christ. Paul's longing was "that I may know Him, and the power of His resurrection."[3] The commitment is to know Him as well as to do what is necessary to get to know Him.

But there is more. Devotional knowledge of the Word is not enough.

Evangelical Christians have institutionalized the study of the Bible. We pay a staff to study and relay Bible truth to the waiting congregation. We install a pastor-priest to interpret Scripture for us. Preaching and exposition of the Bible meet great needs. We must not stop doing them. But the men and women in the pew must never think that secondhand Scripture alone will cause them to grow deep with God.

Most church Bible studies are not Bible studies at all. They are teaching sessions. Pastors I have polled agree that over 95 percent of the people in their congregations never seriously study the Bible. That is, they never take pen and paper and really work through a passage or a topic.

For this reason, Christians remain spiritually anemic. They never progress from milk to solid food.[4] They never wrestle personally with the Word over the doctrines. They accept what is taught. The example of the Bereans should guide them: "Now these were more noble-minded than those in Thessalonica, for they received the word with great eagerness, *examining the Scriptures daily,* to see whether these things were so."[5]

As a young couple just out of college and in our first Air Force assignment, Mary and I looked for a church in the local community. We found one holding a Sunday evening service. As soon as we walked in, we sensed something strange. Later that week the pastor called on us. He stated doctrine that I knew was wrong. He flipped from passage to passage while all I could say was, "I know you are wrong, but I can't show you from Scripture."

At that point I determined to start studying my Bible. I had been reading it, had maintained a devotional time, and knew about doctrine. I had sat under excellent teaching, but I had not really studied the Bible. I was living on secondhand knowledge.

A few months later, I asked Jake Combs of The Navigators to show me how to study a chapter of the Bible. I made a commitment to regularly study Scripture.

I still need it today. Writing, speaking, and my devotional time cannot suffice. I need study, and it needs to be fresh. I have found that I need a small group of people who study the Bible together regularly to motivate me and keep me accountable. We commit to preparing ahead of time and sharing what we have studied.

How is your Bible study? Have you ever made a commitment to *study* the Word?

Your spiritual walk must consist of more than a quiet time and Bible study. Fellowship, obedience, witnessing, and prayer all play their part. But the core is the Bible and the focus on Christ.

NOTES
1. 1 Peter 2:2
2. Many excellent resources are available to help you, such as *Seven Minutes with God, Appointment with God,* and the *Daily Walk,* all available from NavPress, P.O. Box 6000, Colorado Springs, Colorado 80934.
3. Philippians 3:10
4. See Hebrews 5:12-14.
5. Acts 17:11, italics mine

7
Commitment, Materialism, and Success

AND HE SAID TO THEM, "BEWARE, AND
BE ON YOUR GUARD AGAINST EVERY
FORM OF GREED; FOR NOT EVEN WHEN
ONE HAS AN ABUNDANCE DOES
HIS LIFE CONSIST OF
HIS POSSESSIONS."
Luke 12:15

Wealth and success seldom wear well on Christians. Few can handle them with humility and conscientious stewardship. Pitfalls abound. Greed creeps in where once thankfulness reigned.

We live in the midst of a materialistic society. It rubs off on us. Almost unknowingly we make irreversible commitments to a materialistic way of life, and they eat at us like a cancer. Families want bigger houses, so husbands and wives consume their time and energy on houses and things rather than family and outreach. Men and women push for promotion and uproot families for that marginally better job until life becomes a nomadic search for greener pastures. House payments, car payments, and charge card payments—all are binding commitments that lock us into a vicious cycle of life.

In *The Pursuit of God* A.W. Tozer reflects on man's penchant for materialism: "There is within the human heart a tough fibrous root of fallen life whose nature is to possess, always to possess. It covets 'things' with a deep and fierce passion. . . . Things have become necessary to us, a development never originally intended. God's gifts now take the place of God, and the whole course of nature is upset by the monstrous substitutions."[1]

Tozer also reviews how God took one of the richest men alive, Abraham, and brought him to a point of surrender. God asked Abraham for that which he valued most, his son, Isaac. Abraham obeyed implicitly and God chose to rescue Isaac. Abraham at that point "was a man wholly surrendered, a man utterly obedient, a man who *possessed nothing.*"[2]

Wealth and success have never produced lasting happiness, yet even Christians commit their lives to pursuing them.

Jesus told a parable of a rich man in Luke 12:16-21. The rich farmer had a bumper crop, on top of other years of good crops. He decided that he needed more barns. No problem in that. But then he said in his heart, "Soul, you have many goods laid up for many years to come; take your ease, eat, drink and be merry." Then God said, "You fool! This very night your soul is required of you; and now who will own what you have prepared?" Then Jesus applied the principle to us: "So is the man who lays up treasure for himself, and is not rich toward God."

Don't misunderstand the parable. The problem is not riches or building new barns. The problem is the heart attitude, the heart commitment. A life given to wealth and success will turn to ashes and spiritual poverty. According to this parable, the rich man is a fool. Strong language.

Frankly, I get concerned about myself in this regard. Because of speaking engagements and job responsibilities, I fly from place to place—Seattle, Chicago, Singapore, London—a member of the spiritual jet set! Occasionally I find myself thinking I deserve this, and pride creeps in. As I look around at a celebrity-laden Christian culture with Christian heroes and idols, I am concerned about what our value system is becoming, and about what my value system is becoming. In truth, I deserve none of this. I am simply a steward and a servant obligated to use well what God gives in the way of gifts and abilities. I have to ask myself, as Paul asked the Corinthians, "For who regards you as superior? And what do you have that you did not receive? But if you did receive it, why do you boast as if you had not received it?"[3]

Again, the issue is not having wealth or success, but *wanting* either one. The desire corrupts. Timothy was well aware of the dangers when he wrote, "But those who *want* to get rich fall into temptation and a snare and many foolish and harmful desires which plunge men into ruin and destruction."[4]

The pot of gold is never at the end of the rainbow, as is fabled. But Christian men and women still give their lives to its pursuit. Only too late do they realize they have wasted their lives. Solomon, one of the wealthiest men who ever lived, wrote, "Do not weary yourself to gain wealth, cease from your consideration of it. When you set your eyes on it, it is gone. For wealth certainly makes itself wings, like an eagle that flies toward the heavens."[5]

The message is simple. We must not make wealth and success our goals in life.

Should we instead strive for failure and poverty? Hardly. Neither is worthy of lifetime commitment.

You may think that I am opposed to Christians getting rich or reaching positions of power and influence in the world. Not at all: I am simply opposed to that being their overriding goal in life. I am opposed to an emotionally consuming substitution for worthy spiritual goals. I am opposed to the materialistic entrapment so common among Western Christians.

What about the success-oriented teaching that equates God's blessing with material gain and implies that God wants every Christian to be rich? It is from the pit, without biblical evidence. It degrades the sacrifices of martyrs of the past. God's blessing is far beyond material benefits. He *may* bless us materially, but in no way is He *bound* to do so. God is not our puppet. Christians have become accustomed to comfort and success in part because we live in a small dot on the timeline of history where committed Christians are often well received and placed in positions of power. It is a small anomaly in the vast sweep of history. And it will pass.

How does this discussion relate to commitment? I am concerned about the danger of commitment to the wrong things. No commitment to wealth and success will have God's blessing. We simply need a commitment to stewardship of our abilities and resources under God's sovereign guidance—in the perspective of other more vital spiritual commitments.

How do you test where your commitment lies in the matter of possessions? Remember the rich young ruler of Luke 18? His story was not a parable. He was a flesh-and-blood person, and Jesus made it very clear what his commitment should be: "One thing you still lack; sell all that you possess, and distribute it to the poor, and you shall have treasure in heaven; and come, follow Me." The ruler's response was tragic: "But when he had heard these things, he became very sad; for he was extremely rich."[6]

If Jesus made this a condition for you to follow Him, would you? Fill in the blank with some of your possessions: (your name)   , sell your

_____

and give it to the poor.

Would you?

"So we will be brought one by one to the testing place, and we may never know when we are there. At that testing place there will be no dozen possible choices for us; just one and an alternative, but our whole future will be conditioned by the choice we make."[7]

_____

NOTES

1. A.W. Tozer, *The Pursuit of God* (Harrisburg, Pennsylvania: Christian Publications, Inc., 1948), page 22.
2. Tozer, page 27.

3. 1 Corinthians 4:7
4. 1 Timothy 6:9
5. Proverbs 23:4-5
6. Luke 18:22-23
7. Tozer, page 31.

8
Commitment of Your Leisure Time and Personal Privacy

FOR NOT ONE OF US LIVES FOR HIMSELF,
AND NOT ONE DIES FOR HIMSELF;
FOR IF WE LIVE, WE LIVE FOR THE LORD,
OR IF WE DIE, WE DIE FOR THE LORD;
THEREFORE WHETHER WE LIVE OR DIE,
WE ARE THE LORD'S . . . SO THEN
EACH ONE OF US SHALL GIVE ACCOUNT
OF HIMSELF TO GOD.
Romans 14:7-8,12

Have you ever spent an evening or a Saturday with your eyes glued to the television? You should do a dozen things, but you keep gawking at the inane objects wiggling before you. Afterwards, you sense an empty feeling in your stomach knowing you have spent four or five utterly wasted hours and you will never again have those hours back to use. The feeling is even more acute if this is more of a habit than you want to admit.

But we live in a workaholic world. We need space, time, leisure, and recreation. The frantic pace of life infects Christians and non-Christians alike. The non-Christian strives at the job, joins clubs, chooses other recreation, and buys gadgets for his pastimes. He works hard and plays hard. The Christian strives at the job, joins church clubs, pants from one obligation to the other, and then adds the mandatory "super-Christian" activities to his schedule.

So why shouldn't some "wasted" time be allowed? After all, not every minute need be programmed.

The guilty feeling about wasting a few hours comes from the nagging, unspoken question of whether personal discretionary time has purpose.

One of the most significant measures of a person's spiritual commitment is what he does with his discretionary, or leisure, time. Every person has an equal amount of time—168 hours a week. Everyone also has a work commitment, in or out of the home, that seldom exceeds fifty or sixty hours. The remainder of the time demands choices. Television, sports, hobbies, classes, a cabin at the lake, fishing, refurbishing a car, reading, civic activities, and church meetings all consume that extra time. All can be relaxing and beneficial. But do they have purpose, a concentrated focus? A person's devotional time, Bible study, and personal ministry must fit into these hours. But those important things will not happen without the determined commitment of leisure time. There are no automatic saints, no easy ministries.

Before we joined The Navigators, Mary and I found that we had to narrow our interests to have an outreach. I had to cut back on organized sports. Mary had to cut back on her voracious reading and some academic pursuits. The demands of job, four growing children, and a desire to reach out to others spiritually forced us to focus our time. We sacrificed. We experienced some pressured times. We did get tired. But we knew our lives were counting.

An airline pilot I know takes advantage of his flexible schedule to fly a group of Christian evangelists and musicians to places of ministry. He does this at his own cost. Many in his profession run a separate business or focus their time on private hobbies with no thought of ministry.

Dr. Stan Newell, a Seattle podiatrist, takes half a day a week out of revenue-producing appointment hours to allow extra time to study the Bible and think. Herb Stadler has served our church for years on his own time doing maintenance and a multitude of little-noticed tasks. Ed and Betty Bauman have used their home for years for a Bible study for young people. In fact, they built an addition on their house especially for it. Others reach out to their neighbors in small study groups, help the elderly or sick, or give themselves to counseling. And they give up other good pursuits to do these things. They choose. They decide. They make a commitment of their leisure time.

We should not feel guilty when we take leisure time to relax, read a book, watch a quality television program, or "do nothing." We need this. The key test is what portion of discretionary time we spend in this fashion. There awaits no special reward for an absurdly Spartan or masochistic lifestyle. Balance and focus must guide our thinking and actions.

What is the focus of your leisure time? Is it self-serving and inward? Or is it selfless, outward, and committed?

Westerners, particularly Americans, have a fixation on privacy. Fences, locked doors, single-family homes, and private bedrooms relegate us to a minority of privileged people. Our lifestyle is a luxury experienced only by the wealthy few in populous parts of the globe.

But as much as we like, even desire, our solitude, it isolates us from the needs of people. Along with a commitment of leisure time must also come a relinquishing of some of our privacy. Our time is not our own, nor is our lifestyle. It all comes under the leadership of Christ and the focus that He directs.

Committed Christians open the doors of their lives to people. They allow them to invade their privacy and take their time. They let them see into the private rooms of their lives. Their homes are open to people and their schedules adjust to the needs of others. They restrain themselves in their personal liberties. They allow others to influence their choices of recreation and activity.

Three children and a meager budget made private time for Mary and me hard to come by. While working on my Ph.D., we carried on an extensive ministry with students. Even though Mary was recovering from mononucleosis, our home still flooded with people.

One evening near Christmas, we plotted a quiet candlelight dinner in the small living room of our house. The children were in bed and we had just begun this peaceful, romantic time. Then the doorbell rang, and in came one of our student friends. "Hi, whatcha doing? Hey, that looks like a good meal. Don't pay any attention to me. I'll just be here a minute. Brought you some decorations." And he proceeded to put Christmas decorations over the fireplace, whistling as he worked, and chuckling at any amusing comments that Mary and I made to one another.

Discouraging? A little. But yet, that was what we were there for—people and their needs. The years since have produced dozens of such "interruptions"—phone calls, people dropping by, someone with problems, and hundreds of overnight guests. A young Air Force officer brought two hitchhikers to spend the night. My brother found a runaway boy who stayed with us. In our present home we have prepared a special place for guests to stay with us. In the first two and one-half months we lived in this home, the guest area was unoccupied for only five nights.

We get tired. But we have made a commitment to allow people to invade our privacy, and it is worth all the effort. Our children love it. They always have, because we try to include them in our ministry to others. In fact, they bring their friends by the droves (or so it sometimes seems!).

One of the foundational methods of Navigator ministry for over fifty years has been an open home. An open home for hospitality, meetings, and discipling. People live with Navigator staff and observe Christian families in action.

Have you noticed that you can call or impose on some people unannounced and know they will respond positively, whereas you would not approach some others except in the most dire emergency? You may know both kinds of people well, and all are Christians. Which kind of person are you? Do you obey Philippians 2:4: "Do not merely look out for your own personal interests, but also for the interests of others"?

Leisure time, liberty, and privacy—precious commodities. Are you willing to commit them to God for His use?

9
Commitment and Personal Discipline

I PASSED BY THE FIELD OF THE
SLUGGARD, AND BY THE VINEYARD
OF THE MAN LACKING SENSE;
AND BEHOLD, IT WAS COMPLETELY
OVERGROWN WITH THISTLES,
ITS SURFACE WAS COVERED WITH
NETTLES, AND ITS STONE WALL WAS
BEATEN DOWN. WHEN I SAW,
I REFLECTED UPON IT; I LOOKED,
AND RECEIVED INSTRUCTION.
Proverbs 24:30-32

I love the story of the tortoise and the hare.
I can visualize the race. The wily hare, confident
and puffed up, darts from place to place, running
circles around the plodding tortoise. He probably
wore a slick running suit and a pair of earphones
hooked to a cassette player on his belt. The tortoise
plugged along in cut-off jeans and disheveled tennis
shoes. The crowd loved the hare—a thrill a minute
and the sure winner. Everybody loves a winner.
The poor tortoise showed no style, no flair. They
even booed him. But he kept shuffling along . . .
one foot after the other, after the other, after the

other. He never stopped. You know how it ends. The hare dozed off for a quick nap, and the tortoise lumbered across the finish line to win.

I love it! Give me a tortoise any day to ten flashes in the pan who never quite get the job done. I think the reason I like that story so much is that it shows that all the talent and ability in the world are useless without the discipline to point them in the right direction. Someone has said that discipline is the refining fire by which talent becomes ability.

Commitment without discipline is like a luxurious car without gasoline: it looks great, but it's going nowhere. Sincere and earnest commitments are useless without the discipline to carry them out.

Discipline is the ability to say "no" to what is sin, to say "yes" to what is right, and to say "I will" to what ought to be done.

Everyone is highly disciplined in what he or she really wants to do. Young boys will shoot baskets by the hour. Skiers will study and practice with no thought of time spent. Good cooks invest years in perfecting their skills.

Lorne Sanny, president of The Navigators, recently told me, "I have spent my life doing what I *ought* to do, not what I *want* to do." Discipline focuses our abilities to God's ends. Desire focuses our abilities to our ends. A life goal is to make God's "oughts" into our "wants."

The word *discipline* can convey an erroneous idea. We may think of gutting it out, overcoming odds, being tough, having dogged determination, joyless striving, or raw courage. Certainly those phrases communicate aspects of discipline. But other words—biblical words—describe it better:

endurance, self-control, training. Perhaps the best synonym is self-control, one of the fruit of the spirit listed in Galatians 5:23. "Like a city that is broken into and without walls is a man who has no control over his spirit."[1] One mark of a Christian leader is self-control.[2]

The self-controlled person says "no" to sin as it tempts his appetites. He says "yes" to righteousness and "I will" to obedience.

This year I chose Hebrews 12:1-2 as a guiding passage for my personal life:

> Therefore, since we have so great a crowd of witnesses surrounding us, let us also lay aside every encumbrance, and the sin which so easily entangles us, and let us run with endurance the race that is set before us, fixing our eyes on Jesus, the author and perfecter of faith, who for the joy set before Him endured the cross, despising the shame, and has sat down at the right hand of the throne of God.

As I understand this passage, the cloud of witnesses is not a grandstand filled with season-ticket holders, but a coliseum filled with martyrs who set the pace. They ran the race and won. We can picture martyr after martyr whispering, "It was worth it. Keep running. Don't quit."

In the movie *Chariots of Fire,* Eric Liddell is bumped off the track and stumbles and falls in the infield. He gets up, runs his heart out, and wins. Do you have the sense of being in a race? Is there an urgency about your life—a goal that draws you on? Discipline must have a direction. The rules of the race are posted—and they are very simple.

Rule #1: Lay aside every encumbrance (ogkan). A choice. A decision. No one can do it for you. The word *ogkan* could be translated as "a swelling, superfluous flesh." Unneeded weights and encumbrances pile up on our bodies. We see few truly effective Christians. Most are entangled with the weights of the world.

At some point we must decide to strip down and throw aside these weights that keep us from running well. But that requires a specific commitment to do—not just consider. This is the "I will" of discipline.

Rule #2: Lay aside the sin which so easily entangles. Sin, like seeds, always starts small. Which glance of the eye or touch of the hand led my friend to adultery and divorce? Those "little things" grow up to become gross sin. Then they entangle and choke like seaweed. But, again, we must make a conscious choice. We must exercise the "no" of personal discipline.

Rule #3: Run with endurance. When Liddell fell, he got up and kept going. That burst of energy and speed did not come from weeks and years of indolent living. It came from a life of consistent training and discipline. What goes before determines whether a person can endure.

In the earlier Olympic games, the preparation for the events—the training regimen—was as important as the event itself. The competitor could be disqualified by breaking the rules of training as well as by losing in the race itself.

Years of spiritual indolence cannot be made up in moments of religious fervor. The discipline of the past produces the endurance of the present. The practice of spending time in God's Word, prayer, and obedience gives birth to endurance. And endurance begins with a conscious commitment to discipline and self-control.

Rule #4: Fix your eyes on Jesus. We do not endure just to endure, but for a much more noble cause. We endure for the glory of God and for the cause of Christ in the world. Our focus is on the Person of Christ, who endured before us. It is to accomplish His goals, not ours. We do it by a decision to fix—and to keep fixing—our eyes on Christ. It is so easy to run and endure for lesser motives—our own glory, the building of an institution, the acclaim of others.

Each of these rules demands a commitment to a life of personal discipline. Paul said, "I buffet my body and make it my slave, I have preached to others, I myself should be disqualified."

How would you fill in the following statement? "I _____, lest possibly, after _____, I myself should be disqualified."

What commitment do you need to make to keep from being disqualified?

NOTES
1. Proverbs 25:28
2. Titus 1:8
3. 1 Corinthians 9:27

Part Three

Commitment in Your Relationships

10
Commitment and Accountability

IRON SHARPENS IRON,
SO ONE MAN SHARPENS ANOTHER.
Proverbs 27:17

TWO ARE BETTER THAN ONE
BECAUSE THEY HAVE A GOOD RETURN
FOR THEIR LABOR. FOR IF EITHER OF
THEM FALLS, THE ONE WILL LIFT UP
HIS COMPANION. BUT WOE TO THE ONE
WHO FALLS WHEN THERE IS NOT
ANOTHER TO LIFT HIM UP.
Ecclesistes 4:9-10

The glamorized American West produced the image of the macho man. He is a loner—fiercely independent. He is tough, strong, handsome. The capable, independent woman is his female counterpart. Cigarette and liquor ads paint them indelibly in our minds as accountable to no one—totally self-sufficient.

Nothing could be further from the truth. Centuries of human history show that life demands accountability. Few people naturally do what is best for others. In the primitive or frontier past, natural elements held a person accountable to build shelter, gather food, and protect his family. In crowded industrial society, time clocks, pay clerks, foremen, and supervisors enforce accountability. The perverse nature of man tends to sloth, not diligence.

Even our sincere spiritual commitments, privately held, often go silently unfulfilled. And so we become discouraged—even a bit cynical—and hesitate to make new ones.

The only way I know to break this vicious cycle and to keep our commitments is to make ourselves accountable to another person or group. Accountability is foundational to the New Testament concept of fellowship. But it rarely exists in the church body today. We have emaciated the meaning of fellowship in our efforts to make Christianity more appealing and acceptable to a sophisticated world.

Biblical fellowship cannot exist without the elements of "stimulating one another to love and good deeds," seeing that no one comes short of the grace of God."[1] "Those who continue in sin, rebuke in the presence of all," and "bear one another's burdens."[2]

Paul held Peter accountable for his actions. The Jerusalem Council held Paul accountable. Titus was accountable to Paul for appointing elders in Crete. Even Jesus was accountable to the Father for His actions.

We all need other people to help us keep our commitments, but only if we are serious about keeping them. God forbid that we should get in the habit of making commitments with no intention of keeping them.

How do we make ourselves accountable to

someone? Do we walk up to an aquaintance in church and say, "I've just made a commitment to God to stop cheating in my business. Will you check up on me?" Or do we get up in church and vaguely ask, "Would you pray for me in a commitment I have made to the Lord?" Neither is quite appropriate.

We must ask: Accountability *for what* and *to whom*?

We need accountability for our personal lives, our ministries, and our families. Of the three, personal life accountability is most crucial, since the latter two are more visible. Personal life could include such things as quiet time, prayer, Scripture memory, Bible study, a sin or habit we are trying to conquer, exercise, witnessing—or any other areas of personal need God brings to mind.

It would be ludicrous to have someone hold us accountable in twenty areas of our personal life. It would be like running through a preflight checklist in an airplane—necessary, but boring. Pick one or two areas of special need. Keep track of the others yourself. The act of accountable discipline in one area surprisingly spills over into other areas of life.

For example, suppose you had made a commitment to have a fifteen-minute daily quiet time, reading the Bible and praying. Ask a friend to check with you weekly on the specifics. How many quiet times did you have and for how long? Don't let him be easy on you by saying, "Well, how did it go this week?" And don't give a noncommittal response such as, "Well, not too bad, but I could do better." Be specific.

For ministry, most people need some urging to be involved in evangelism, Bible study, or discipling.

The best commitment is to be involved with other people in some type of ministry. Specifics on such commitments are discussed in a later chapter.

In your family, the key is to be committed to meeting the needs of your spouse and children. Depending on your tendencies and history, you may need more or less accountability to follow through in this area. Again, more on this in chapters to come.

To whom should we make ourselves accountable? I would like to say the church. But it won't work. By the time the church as a body becomes aware of personal needs, it is most often too late. Accountability needs to be to a person—your spouse or a close friend.

Accountability also can occur in a small group. Such accountability can be very effective for everyone involved. Two are better than one. One person does sharpen the life of another. If your commitments are sincere, why not include the insurance to bring them to reality by adding accountability to the commitment?

Accountability puts teeth into commitment. And it forces you to open up an area of your life to scrutiny by another. Not everyone is willing to do that—to take the risk of revealing the inner life. In doing so, we are not quite so independent and self-sufficient. Accountability puts pressure on us to perform, and opens the door to failure. But the rewards fully outweigh the risks. Consider the great sense of accomplishment as spiritual commitments become reality.

NOTES
1. Hebrews 10:24-25 and 12:15
2. 1 Timothy 5:20, Galatians 6:2

11
Commitment to Your Marriage

I TAKE THEE . . . IN SICKNESS AND
IN HEALTH, FOR RICHER, FOR POORER,
'TIL DEATH DO US PART.
Traditional Marriage Vow

Of course, today, not many use the traditional marriage vow. Nor, it seems, do many keep it. Even for many Christians, the marriage bond has lost its strength. It is a disposable Band-Aid. I hear many excuses for breaking that sacred commitment:

"I can't stand her any more."

"He never really loved me."

"We never could communicate."

"We respect each other too much to stay together."

Feeble excuses. True, perhaps, but still no reason for divorce.

For many, the issue becomes adultery, or at least another person who displaces the affections in the heart of one of the partners. And that is called sin. Not a feeble excuse—an enormous barrier.

The ultimate glue in a marriage is not love, sex, an emotional feeling, children, or law. It is commitment, the conscious decision to stay together and make it work. It derives from those first vows to give yourself unreservedly to that one person. It rejects the accepted social ruse of sequential polygamy.

But is not the issue more complex? Is not a glibly stated "Be committed!" a simplistic view of a complicated issue, especially from someone who has a happy marriage? Yes. The problems of marriage cannot be solved by shouted simplicities.

In Henry Fonda's last television production before his death, he and his co-star portrayed an elderly couple reviewing their lifetime together. "Summer Solstice" flashed over the tensions and even the infidelity of their early years. In the wedding scene, the bride refused to say the vow because it contained the word *obey* and was different from the groom's vow. After an animated conference before a flustered minister, they vowed to accept each other "as is." In old age the wife asked Fonda why he didn't divorce her. He thought for some time and simply said, "Because of our vow."

That is a secular statement. But it has merit. The vow—the commitment—must mean something to both husband and wife.

From the beginning, God intended a permanent, committed union in marriage. "For this cause a man shall leave his father and his mother, and shall cleave to his wife; and they shall become one flesh."[1] Jesus added to that by saying, "What therefore God has joined together, let no man separate."[2]

In our own marriage, Mary and I have agreed from the beginning, and reaffirmed often, that divorce is never an option. It is never to be discussed, much less contemplated. One wife was asked if she ever considered divorcing her popular and rather insensitive husband. She replied, "No. Murder, maybe. But divorce, no."

It seems that a series of commitments are necessary to make a marriage last. Let me suggest a few.

An initial commitment or a renewing of that absolute commitment to stay in the marriage no matter what. It's not always easy. Many incidents take place to test that commitment—harsh words that cannot be taken back, actions that flout the commitment, and incidents that never seem to die.

Mary and I once knew a Christian wife whose husband was an unbeliever. But he was more than that; he was proud, arrogant, unthoughtful, demanding, and even unfaithful. However, she stuck it out. Tears, anger, and desperation challenged her commitment, but she determined to stay as long as he would allow her. He is still the same. But the last page of that marriage has not been written yet.

A commitment to remain faithful in mind and body. Sexual unfaithfulness never happens on a whim. The mind conceives the act months and years before, awaiting only the opportunity. All the excuses of a miserable physical relationship or lack of communication cannot justify marital infidelity. A basic commitment to mental and physical fidelity must be made.[3] This is a decision, a choice, an act of the will. "Let marriage be held in honor among all, and let the marriage bed be undefiled."[4]

A commitment to love your spouse. People *fall* in love, but they decide to *stay* in love. Emotions change like the weather, but love must be a determined commitment. "Husbands, love your wives, just as Christ also loved the church."[5] "Encourage the young women to love their husbands."[6] We must commit to love in a self-sacrificial way whether or not the love is reciprocated.

A commitment to work on your marriage. No marriage can stand neglect and still survive. But in the panic of climbing the company ladder, accumulating "things," and raising children, we can easily neglect paying attention to our marriage relationship. Any auto mechanic will tell you that maintenance, not repair, is the key to lengthening the life of a car. We dare not neglect the maintenance of our marriage. Repairs are costly and not always effective. Commit yourself to work on your marriage as a way of life. J. Alan Peterson, in his book *The Myth of the Greener Grass,* masterfully shows in story after story the painful result of neglect in a marriage and the consequent magnetic pull to another person of the opposite sex who will listen and empathize.[7]

This is not a marriage manual, but a challenge to commitment in the second most vital relationship of our lives. Commitment may be impossible, especially in a troubled marriage, without a more basic commitment. This basic commitment is to the lordship of Christ in your personal life and the belief that God has your best interests at heart. As you wander from your walk with God, you will also wander from your vow to your mate. God's overwhelming love for you is the only fire to ignite and keep burning to insure your love for your spouse.

I strongly recommend the book by Lawrence J. Crabb, Jr. entitled *The Marriage Builder.* He expertly describes the mandatory building blocks for oneness in marriage—grace, commitment, and acceptance. I have focused on the second. He pleads the grace of God for the power of God in the marriage. Dr. Crabb sees allowing Christ to be the fulfillment of your deepest longings and desires as a necessary prerequisite to marriage fulfillment. Your spouse can never meet your deepest longings and desires. Only Christ can do that.

In his discussion of commitment, Crabb makes two excellent points: "Point 1: The basis for true commitment is the goodness of God. Point 2: Honoring commitments because of a profound trust in God's goodness will feel less like 'doing one's duty' and more like pursuing one's deepest desires."[8]

In the cliché of a few decades ago, "It takes two to tango!" The marriage commitment rests on a two-way covenant. One cannot force another to do or be other than that which he or she chooses. But even God loved when there was no love in return. We keep our part of the covenant regardless of the response.

Many who read this have already experienced the bitterness of divorce and are in another marriage. You cannot relive history. Lessons must be learned, restitution made, forgiveness asked, and responsibilities fulfilled, but you must live where you are now. Make those vital commitments now to build a solid foundation for the years ahead. It is never too late to know God's good plan for your life.

Others who read this are experiencing a living hell in their marriages. As you review this short chapter, what commitments are missing? Don't neglect your own commitment to Christ's lordship. Discuss your commitments and begin to rebuild. You can. In fact, you must.

NOTES
1. Genesis 2:24
2. Matthew 19:6
3. See *Honesty, Morality,* and *Conscience* by Jerry White (Colorado Springs, Colorado: NavPress, 1978), pages 192-194.
4. Hebrews 13:4
5. Ephesians 5:25
6. Titus 2:4
7. Tyndale House Publishers, Inc., 1983
8. Lawrence J. Crabb, Jr., *The Marriage Builder* (Grand Rapids, Michigan: Zondervan Publishing House, 1982), pages 113, 116.

12
Commitment to Your Children

BEHOLD, CHILDREN ARE A GIFT
OF THE LORD; THE FRUIT OF
THE WOMB IS A REWARD.
Psalm 127:3

Regret.

A sad word. A worse feeling.

Regret describes the gut feeling of many parents as they watch their children slip away from their conscious control—regret for what they could have done, should have done, and now want to do, but it's too late. Some children rebel. Some smile sweetly and do their own thing. Some run. And some become godly men and women in spite of their parents' mistakes.

I have felt some of those regrets. I still do when I think back on my fathering in the early years of our marriage. My job in the space program at Cape Canaveral was exciting. I was driven by career, Bible studies, hobbies, and sports. When our first two children were born, it was as though I said, "Isn't that nice. Mary, you take good care of them. Let me know if you need anything."

What a blind misconception of parenting. Earlier I mentioned a commitment I made to spend time daily with God. At the same time, God spoke to me about my children and family. It was a spiritual turning point in my life.

I made a personal commitment to do two things: first, to spend time daily playing with the children; second, to allow them to interrupt me at any time. To this day, when any child calls, my secretary knows to interrupt me no matter what I am doing or who I am meeting with. I still have difficulty being "too busy," but I have consciously worked at my availability to them.

Children are both a gift from God and a sacred trust. They are a human responsibility second only to our marriage relationship. With no one else do we bear such a far-reaching responsibility. Every parent becomes a master teacher with no professional training whatsoever. The influence on a child is pervasive. As a daughter blooms into womanhood or a son punches his way through adolescence to manhood, we see an incredible replica of ourselves in voice and body, strengths and faults. They learn even when we do not intend to teach.

The easy part is the command to provide— diapers, food, shelter, and clothing. These come naturally to most parents. But teaching is quite another thing. If only human parents were more like animals in the wild, who automatically teach their young how to live and survive. The human parent must consciously choose to do this.

"And these words, which I am commanding you today, shall be on your heart; and you shall teach them diligently to your sons and shall talk of them when you sit in your house and when you walk by the way and when you lie down and when you rise up."[1] What other time is there? The charge to teach and train our children cannot be delegated to a school, a church, or a babysitter.

It is a charge that demands clear commitment. It will not just happen. The commitment to love, teach, train, and provide must be shared by both parents. In one-parent homes, God will make special provision for those needs as the parent fully accepts the responsibility.

But, like every commitment, there is a cost. It involves time, emotional and physical energy, and money. Fathers may need to turn down a promotion or restrict their travel to make time for the children. Mothers may need to forsake their own careers for a time or live with less in the way of a home. Some hard choices will need to be made.

As I reflected on which specific commitments must be made regarding our children, two were basic:
1. A commitment to make time for the children;
2. A commitment to personally take the responsibility for their spiritual teaching and training.

Children are incredible time consumers. From incessant diapers, incessant feedings, can't-wait-toddler attention, frantic demands of self-centered grade schoolers, and demands for taxi service to nervous waiting after they begin to drive, years of time seem crunched into weeks. It never lets up. There is no urgency like that of a child or a teen with a "need." But some day you will long for those captive times of influence with them. Make the most of them while you can.

The commitment to teach and train requires a conscious plan. Time demands will constantly be there. But most children do not demand teaching, even with their incredible ability to ask questions.

We need a plan to teach spiritual truth, social skills, privileges of living, and moral precepts. Children need more than just a dinner prayer or a hurried devotion. We must decide on things to communicate, and take advantage of every situation to teach. Mary has been the creative planner in our family in this regard. She has recorded many means of fulfilling this commitment in her book *Growing Together: Building Your Family's Spiritual Life.* (NavPress, 1981).

Finally, we must let our children go. This is a commitment in itself. Both Mary and I have been grateful to our parents for their sensitivity in truly "letting us go." They have never tried to control us as adults, but have always been there for counsel. We crossed that line into a new relationship with hardly a bump. In many cases that was not so easy.

It was hard to let you go:
To watch womanhood reach out and snatch you
Long before the mothering was done.
But if God listened to mothers and gave in,
Would the time for turning loose of daughters
ever come?

It was hard when you went away—
For how was I to know
The serendipity of letting go
Would be seeing you come home again
And meeting in a new way
Woman to woman—
Friend to friend.[2]

Marilee Zdenek

Finally, when you have done all you can, your children will make their own choices—and commitments.

Are you doing all you can now?

NOTES
1. Deuteronomy 6:6-7
2. Marilee Zdenek, *Splinters in My Pride* (Waco, Texas: Word Books, 1979), part 1.

13
Commitment to Leadership and Authority

OBEY YOUR LEADERS, AND
SUBMIT TO THEM; FOR THEY KEEP
WATCH OVER YOUR SOULS, AS THOSE
WHO WILL GIVE AN ACCOUNT.
LET THEM DO THIS WITH JOY AND
NOT WITH GRIEF, FOR THIS WOULD
BE UNPROFITABLE FOR YOU.
Hebrews 13:17

David, the shepherd who was anointed king but hired as a servant, was playing his harp in King Saul's presence, trying to soothe the mad king. In a fit of irrational rage, Saul picked up a spear and hurled it at David. He missed and David ran. This was the second time Saul's jealous madness had pushed him to kill David. Plot after plot failed in Saul's attempts to murder him.

Finally David escaped to the mountains. Saul relentlessly pursued. In the next months of desperate pursuit and escape, David had a perfect opportunity to kill Saul—seemingly God-given.

After all, the people loved David. Samuel's anointing had declared him the next king. Why not kill Saul? David explained it to his puzzled, grizzled mob of fugitives: "Far be it from me because of the Lord that I should do this thing to my lord, the Lord's anointed, to stretch out my hand against him, since he is the Lord's anointed."[1]

We will never know what kind of king David would have been had he killed Saul then. We do know he became a man after God's own heart.

Interestingly, God did not suddenly say to David, "You did right. You've passed the test. Just relax and I'll take care of Saul myself." Instead, David was driven out of the country. He despaired. He hid. He even acted as though he were insane. Things got worse, not better. He had a second chance to kill Saul and refused again (See 1 Samuel 26).

What strange behavior for a great leader. David was an unusual man, one who knew both how to be *under* authority and how to be *in* authority.[2]

Two classes of authority affect all of us: secular and spiritual. Secular authorities include employers, national government, and local civil government.[3] Spiritual authorities include pastors, elders, leaders of lay movements, and the family structure. In each case, the authority can be just or unjust, competent or incompetent.

Christians certainly need to be committed to living under proper civil and vocational authorities. Yet many Christians bristle under any infringement of their freedom and spend much of their lives being bitter and angry toward authority. This attitude carries over into the Christian community—and it is poison to the body.

The cause of Christ in the world desperately needs godly leadership. But leaders need followers. Coaches need teams. Great tasks need willing workers. All of these require the exercise of submission to authority, and that is a bad word in Christian circles. *Fellowship, team, body, relationships, love, outreach*, and dozens of other warm terms capture acceptance. But not *authority*. Leadership is acceptable, but only after careful scrutiny, long testing, and assurances that the followers are really independent.

The danger of unjust leadership in Christian circles is not really so great. Certainly there are a few who purposely misuse their position and influence. But most problems arise from simple incompetence. However, even an incompetent, godly leader with committed followers can accomplish much in the kingdom of God. Gideon, Jacob, Saul, Peter, and Thomas were not all that competent—yet God used them.

The greatest difference between secular and spiritual authority lies in mandatory versus voluntary submission. In the secular realm, money, security, position, and law all marshal power to make authority effective. In the spiritual realm, all submission is voluntary and often erratic.

A critical turning point in the life of a growing believer occurs when a deep commitment is made to place oneself under the authority of others in life and ministry. Not blind submission. The Bible has no place for that: "Remember those who led you, who spoke the word of God to you; and *considering the outcome of their way of life,* imitate their faith."[4]

We always evaluate. Evaluation does not mean constant criticism. Every leader will make mistakes and no one will lead perfectly. Most of us do not want to lead, but we often want to critique how another leads. I appreciate Theodore Roosevelt's viewpoint:

> It is not the critic who counts. The credit actually belongs to the man in the arena, whose face is marred by dust and sweat and blood—who at best knows in the end the triumph of high achievement, and who at worst, if he fails at least fails while daring greatly, so that his place will never be with those cold and timid souls who know neither victory nor defeat.

Let us be among those who are in the battle, not those who criticize those who lead into battle.

Most Christians place themselves under no authority except perhaps that of the church through membership. The Church in the world engages in constant battle with the forces of darkness. No battle is ever waged by wishing. It needs people who pray, plan, and act together. There are no effective loners.

When I speak of commitment to leadership and authority, I do not mean commitment to only one authority—that is dictatorship. We always have multiple commitments and multiple leaders. Our pastor, the leader of a women's study, the young couples team leader, the chairman of the church outreach committee, the husband, the parent—all constitute legitimate authorities.

Few commitments to authority are permanent.

They are for a season, for a task, for a need. No human authority is unlimited and no commitment is unconditional. Commitment should be made not only to a leader, but also to a task. They go hand in hand. A leader without a task has no purpose. A task without a leader flounders and fails.

The danger for most Christians is not committing to the wrong task or leader, but making no commitment at all, and bristling with indignation when any authority attempts to enlist them.

I believe the cause of Christ lurches along like a temperamental engine, misfiring and quitting, largely because we never know who the real soldiers are. The leader blows the trumpet and wonders who will decide to come to battle.

I have observed many gifted men and women who never learned to function under authority. They wanted their independence and their options. They never learned the lesson of the Roman commander who told Christ that he was also "a man under authority."[5] Invariably I see them fall into spiritual mediocrity, for no one will follow them either.

Take the risk. Counter your independence. Put yourself under authority. Commit to it.

NOTES
1. 1 Samuel 24:6
2. For an excellent discussion of authority, see *A Tale of Three Kings,* by Gene Edwards (Christian Books, P.O. Box 1092, Goleta, CA 93116).
3. For further discussion, see *Your Job: Survival or Satisfaction?,* by Jerry and Mary White (Zondervan, 1977).
4. Hebrews 13:7, italics mine
5. Matthew 8:9

14
Commitment and Your Ministry

BUT YOU [TIMOTHY], BE SOBER
IN ALL THINGS, ENDURE HARDSHIP,
DO THE WORK OF AN EVANGELIST,
FULFILL YOUR MINISTRY.
2 Timothy 4:5

A heresy is afoot in the Christian community. It is this: ordinary lay men and women are not under the same obligation to have a ministry as certain gifted people. It seems that deeply committed lay people are such a rarity that they are elevated almost to the level of a pastor (not quite, of course). In fact, as these few give themselves to evangelism or teaching or discipling, the following comment invariably surfaces: "He really ought to be in the full-time ministry."

It's strange. Others never seem to think that they should also have a personal ministry

There are a few gifted people with great capacity.
Some apply their gifts and capacity to ministry.
Others apply theirs to work or hobbies. But mostly
there are just average people—some of whom allow
themselves to be significantly used by God. And
they do it at great cost to themselves. The cost is
the infringement on their leisure time, their personal choices, and their private lives.

Why don't more people see themselves as
having a personal ministry? Part of the problem
is a caricature of what the term *ministry* means.
The mind conjures up images of preaching from the
pulpit, a missionary in Africa, seminary training,
or any number of classic pastoral duties. To minister
simply means to serve. Ministry is meeting the
needs of people—reaching out to non-Christians
and Christians alike. Only a minuscule percentage
of true ministry is done by the professionals. The
vast majority is done by ordinary people. There is
no New Testament distinction between secular and
sacred. True ministry is done twenty-four hours a
day by all believers—if they are committed. They
minister on the job, in their neighborhood, in their
city, and in their church.

Ordinary people doing ordinary acts of service.
Person after person comes to my mind's eye as I
review the past.

Bill Anderson, a milkman, gave himself weekly
to young boys in our church through the Christian
Service Brigade group. My friend of over thirty
years, Bud Ponten, grew up with cerebral palsy and
overcame speech and body handicaps that would
discourage most people. Yet he constantly reached
out to junior and senior high students. I still have

notes from his Sunday school class. As I worked with him in his printing shop, I always sensed that he had a far greater purpose in life than just printing.

Bill Forland came to know Christ in his fifties. He now gives himself unreservedly to several significant ministries, refusing to sit back and enjoy his early retirement from the company he founded.

Zeke Easley used his executive position in a prestigious company to influence top executives to hear the Gospel and consider the claims of Christ. He was one of the key leaders to challenge the ban of a religious speaker from a secular campus in his city. He just keeps pushing for people to hear the Gospel.

Cec Davidson, a navy electronics mate in World War II, and his wife, Thelma, keep having young servicemen in their home for discipling. In over thirty years as Navigator staff, Cec and Thelma have influenced hundreds of lives.

After the Korean war, an ordinary young Marine, Ron York, returned to Idaho, intent on hunting and fishing. A friend asked him to go to a conference in Colorado. The decision changed his life. He has been used by God for many years in Asia in a Navigator discipling ministry.

Les, an agriculture major in college, has worked in a Marxist country for years through difficult times. He keeps plugging away at terracing farms, digging wells for irrigation, and discipling a few key men and women.

Our dear friend Frances McCarthy, ill and in pain for years, shares Christ wherever she goes. Recently she had a suspected heart attack and was being taken to the hospital in an ambulance. The attendant said, "Don't worry, Mrs. McCarthy. You'll be okay." She replied, "Oh, I'm not worried. You see, I know where I'm going." And she shared the Gospel with the young ambulance attendant. She never quits.

William Carey, an ordinary shoemaker, had the world on his heart and unknowingly became the father of the modern missionary movement.

Bob Shepler, a young businessman, invested his spare time in rounding up young fifth to seventh-grade boys for his Sunday school class in the community center of a post-war housing project—and taking them fishing, swimming, and hiking. I came to know Christ in that class.

Every day an elderly retired preacher in his eighties put on his three-piece suit and hat and walked sprightly through the neighborhood handing out gospel tracts and talking to anyone who would listen. He repeatedly gave tracts to the same young boys who laughed behind his back. He was not about to waste away, sitting disheveled in front of a television. He was doing what he could.

Fred Hignell III, a developer in California, focuses his life in both evangelism and discipling in his business community. Chris Canlis uses his well-known restaurant as a platform to witness and disciple others. He believes God put him there for that purpose.

Others tend baby nurseries, teach young children, visit the sick, do errands for the elderly, open their homes to Bible classes, and do administrative tasks.

All these people are ordinary people who decided to focus on doing one thing well. That is another key to ministry—focusing your efforts.

Ordinary people don't usually flash to the front. They have to focus to count. They don't serve on five committees and say yes to every request. They make a decision on what the focus of their efforts in ministry should be and stick to it, much to the consternation of the activity organizers and program planners.

Paul's "this one thing I do," rather than "these many things I dabble at," becomes a necessary by-word for the person who has a personal ministry.

We all need that—a focus, a purpose, a calling. This gives a deep sense of contribution to life. And, if practiced with disciplined restraint from activities for activities' sake, it will not result in a frenzied, out-of-balance lifestyle with no time for family. In fact, a focused life results in more time rather than less.

Ordinary people with a *focused task.* There is power in that combination. But the power comes only when those ordinary people make real commitments to focus their lives in a ministry.

15
Commitment and Your Church

NOT FORSAKING OUR OWN
ASSEMBLING TOGETHER, AS IS THE
HABIT OF SOME BUT ENCOURAGING
ONE ANOTHER; AND ALL THE MORE,
AS YOU SEE THE DAY DRAWING NEAR.
Hebrews 10:25

Dusk was fast approaching in the small Middle Eastern village. Work was done and people were gathering with their families around the evening meal. The Jews and Romans alike called a truce for this quiet time. But in the shadows, a few figures slipped into a house, careful not to be observed. They gathered to break bread, to sing quietly, to fellowship around the risen Christ. A church was meeting. Two of their number had been threatened last week, and one lost his job. But they rejoiced together and shared with those in need.

Century after century the faithful have often

met in an atmosphere of hostility and pressure. Even today scenes like this are repeated in Eastern European countries. Meeting incurs risk. The believers have carefully counted the cost of involvement in their church. And they count the risk for meaningful fellowship well worth it. They are part of a vision and a mission operating not as a congregation or a system, but a body.

In America and many other parts of the world, the cost is little more than missing a favorite television program. Is there no commitment where there is no cost?

As I have watched the parade of people through our church, and other churches, I wonder why so few commit themselves to a local body of believers in a significant way. Many sit and soak and do little else, and they flee at the first sign of trouble or pressure. They fail to become involved or to give; the priority for corporate worship falls far down the list. They criticize all that is wrong with a specific local congregation.

Underneath the restlessness of the typical evangelical church lies a root of non-commitment and an inward focus totally uncharacteristic of the early Church. The problem is not a lack of godly pastors and staff, or the presence of inept leadership. The problem is in the pew and ultimately in the atmosphere of the evangelical constituency.

The American passion for excitement invades the church. A generation raised on thrilling movies, dynamic television programs, and professional sports becomes bored with an "ordinary" church. The demand for platform entertainment, exciting programs, and stellar preaching seems far removed from those small bands of early Christians and more like the institutionalized cathedral Christianity of the Middle Ages.

There is a sickness in what I call "the fickleness of the floaters." There are people who go where the action is, or where the problems aren't. I know of one instance in which a couple left and rejoined a church three times, even serving on the board at one time. I see so many who back out when the going gets tough—when the pastor is not preaching superbly or the congregation becomes hostile or divided. Many live on the fringes, lobbing salvos of criticism when difficulties arise. Others analyze the church like the stock market, buying in as it goes up and selling out when it goes down. I see the struggle of entertainment versus worship and of a theater versus simply a place to meet. In the midst are the shifting sands of evangelicals—now you see them, now you don't.

The super-churches and the super-pastors cannot be the norm. I applaud their existence and their influence. But the vast majority of churches are not like that. Where are the super-churches in the slums of Chicago or the ethnic neighborhoods of Los Angeles?

What can we do besides comment or complain? We need to accept the challenge to commit ourselves to responsible membership. This responsible membership includes a positive attitude, involvement, and loyalty, all backed by commitment, a commodity often in short supply. But what kind of commitment?

Our *attitude* toward the local church is the first level of commitment. A local body of believers, with all its imperfections, is still the major expression of Christ's witness on earth. In its many forms it gathers for worship, teaching, and fellowship. And it is biblical. We are to be a part of it, not loners. We may see its human problems, but our attitude must be that God will use it, and use us in its midst. We need an expectant attitude that expresses confidence rather than doubt. We change our attitude by an act of the will. We *decide* to view our church as a body ordained by God for a purpose, and believe that He will use it.

The next step is *involvement*. We need to be a part of a church, not bystanders. We need to be there. Let's not belittle the importance of simple attendance. If the Rotary Club can elicit a commitment from thousands of businessmen to be present weekly, surely the church can also.

Corporate worship is not enough. We really get to know people in the context of a Sunday school class and a smaller segment of the church. In your involvement, support those activities that are meaningful both to you and to the central purpose of the church. You cannot, and should not, be involved in every program. Measure your involvement to be effective. But get involved! Don't sit on the sidelines.

Finally, there is *loyalty*. When we criticize our church, we criticize ourselves. The one who has the right to criticize is the one who pitches in and works. Be loyal to the pastor and staff. If they have needs, go to them directly. Do not sow seeds of discontent or become a troublemaker. And above all, don't run when trouble and difficulties develop. Be part of the solution.

In an individualistic Western society, we tend

to think only of the witness of a person, not a group. The apostle Paul wrote to the Thessalonians and commended them for the impact of their entire church:

> You also became imitators of us and of the Lord,
> having received the word in much tribulation with
> the joy of the Holy Spirit, so that you became
> an example to all the believers in Macedonia
> and in Achaia. For the word of the Lord has
> sounded forth from you, not only in Macedonia
> and Achaia, but also in every place your faith
> toward God has gone forth, so that we have no
> need to say anything.[1]

The entire church upheld the reputation of the entire church. We have much to learn from Asian societies where group functioning and loyalty are high ideals. When we look for a church, let's not look for what we can get, but what we can give.

Make a commitment before God to be a responsible part of your local body.

NOTES
1. 1 Thessalonians 1:6-8

Part Four
The Practice of Commitment

16
Commitment to a Vision, a Calling, and the World

THEN THEY SAID, "LET US ARISE AND
BUILD." SO THEY PUT THEIR HANDS
TO THE GOOD WORK.
Nehemiah 2:18

The stillness of the Middle Eastern night was about complete, except for a faint crunching of slow footsteps in sand. The stars were spectacular, flashing in a way that signaled the immensity of the universe. A not-quite-full moon lighted the countryside, throwing heavy shadows to the west. It was idyllic except for the scene it illuminated. Dark shadows fell from piles of rubble interspersed with charred remains of wood and metal. Huge stones lay crazily tipped over one another. The ruin went as far as the eye could see in all directions.

A man leading a donkey slowly picked his way

through the rubble. Now and then he stopped to look around, then moved on to another place. He was middle-aged, with dark hair and beard tinged with an early gray. In good light it would have been apparent that he was out of place. His robe was of high quality, unlike those worn by the scruffy inhabitants of this burned-out city. The air bore a desert coolness, but still sweat came off his forehead and ran down his cheek. Or it may have been tears. He paused at the remains of a large gate bearing the bent symbol of the once-proud city. As it had before, fear gripped the man as he recalled those few days of panic and indecision.

My life as a foreigner had taken a very pleasant turn. I had become a trusted confidant of King Artaxerxes. As his official cupbearer, I guarded his life daily. As a Jew, I loyally sought news of Jerusalem for my friends since I was in the center of communication of the kingdom. When word came of the destroyed walls, I was deeply moved, to my surprise. I wept and fasted for days and was moved to pray.

A plan began to form in my mind, which sent great fear through my entire body. The memory of that spiritual struggle will never leave me. I argued with God: "Why me? The king will kill me. Others can do it. My family is doing so well."

But I finally told God I would obey. Days and nights of fasting and struggle had left me haggard and tired. And I was despondent as well as fearful. Yet I knew I must go and ask the king to allow me to go to rebuild the wall of my ancestors' city. Absurd. Why me?

Nehemiah shuddered as he recalled the next day.

I went to the king. He saw my drawn face and asked what was wrong. My stomach twisted with fear. No one, absolutely no one, was to be sad in this Oriental king's presence. Death was sure to follow. I told him, "Let the king live forever. Why should my face not be sad when the city, the place of my fathers' tombs, lies desolate and its gates have been consumed by fire?" The king asked what I requested. I quietly prayed to God and then asked that the king send me to rebuild the walls of Jerusalem. I remember my heart pounding as I asked the unthinkable—letters of safe passage as well as materials. He granted them. I didn't sleep for two days from the shock and excitement and some fear as to what I had committed myself to do. God's hand was on me.

Even now in this still, cool night Nehemiah's face flushed with the memory. But he was here now in a hostile environment with yet no support. He circled the desolate city. Tomorrow was the day of confrontation.

He gathered the leaders and told them how God had led. Then they said, "Let us arise and build."[1] And they did. Later there was opposition, disagreement, and sin on the part of the leaders. Nehemiah confronted them. Once he even struck them and pulled out their hair! But the task was done in fifty-two days. A miracle.

What drove Nehemiah to such leadership and risk? He had few needs. He was comfortable. Why did he get involved?

God brought the plight of Jerusalem to his attention and gave him a burning *vision* as to the need: Rebuild the walls. Then God gave him a specific *calling* to do it. Finally, Nehemiah saw the significance of this task to his whole nation, and the known *world*.

Vision is the central driving force of a Christian's life. Like an internal combustion engine where an explosion of gas transfers power to the piston and to the drive shaft, so vision gives power to the Christian. This is a different power than that of the Holy Spirit. The Holy Spirit empowers the Christian to live a holy, godly life. The vision from God empowers a Christian to live a fruitful, devoted life. Certainly God wants us to be holy. But a holy life without holy vision ultimately leads to inward spiritual poverty. The ascetic or monkish life can lead to a selfish grasping for spiritual experience. Without the driving power of vision, such a life perverts the outward fruitfulness of a godly life. Spirituality without vision leads to a life without focus, and motion without direction.

The central vision for every Christian is the Great Commission: "Go therefore and make disciples of all the nations, baptizing them in the name of the Father and the Son and the Holy Spirit, teaching them to observe all that I commanded you; and lo, I am with you always, even to the end of the age."[2] There is no other commission. Jesus' commandment is the compelling vision of all believers. To reach every person in our generation with the Gospel of Jesus Christ, beginning where we live and work, is the central task of each believer. Only with a commitment to that vision can our lives have true meaning. It is the task of the entire body of Christ, not just one person. Each of us has a part in accomplishing the vision of the whole body, yet the vision of the whole must drive each person.

Jesus set His face to the cross with the vision for the redemption of all mankind. Paul's part in the Great Commission was a vision to reach the Gentiles.

Vision needs a vehicle for practical expression. This is our *calling*. In this sense, calling is distinct from the primary biblical usage of a calling to salvation. It is, rather, the specific task to which God calls us as our part in fulfilling the Great Commission. This task relates to our spiritual gifts and abilities. It is the action part of our vision.

Jesus' command was, "I chose you, and appointed you, that you should go and bear fruit."[3] The action was to *go* and *bear fruit.* Earlier He said, "Lift up your eyes, and look on the fields, that they are white for harvest. . . . I sent you to reap."[4] Look and reap. Seeing is the vision. Reaping is the calling. Commitment to action always accompanies the imparting of vision.

Isaiah's holy vision of the Lord moved him to respond, "Here am I. Send me!"[5] God responded, "Go, and tell this people."[6] Paul met Christ on the road to Damascus and was sent to the Gentiles "to open their eyes so that they may turn from darkness to light and from the dominion of Satan to God, in order that they may receive forgiveness of sins and an inheritance among those who have been sanctified by faith in Me."[7]

Many believers know the Great Commission, but do not sense its compelling vision. Agreement theologically does not lead to committed action. Some believers talk vision, listen to speakers, and even weep—but *do* nothing. They assent to no calling. Commitment to a vision requires commitment to a calling.

The specific task in one's calling may vary greatly. Some support evangelists, disciplers, or teachers. Some are directly involved in these tasks. But all are still responsible to evangelize where they live and work. The key is knowing what *you* are to do. It could be working with children, the elderly, young people, or counseling. One person cannot do everything. But every person can do something. Let no one be guilty of doing nothing.

Vision and *calling*, though indispensable to a focused life, need the perspective of the *world* to be complete. We need bifocal vision. We experience the dynamics of the Great Commission personally where we live and work and in our nation. But our distant vision must focus on the world—all nations. Jesus meant what He said. We must keep our bifocal vision on our "Jerusalem" and "the remotest part of the earth."[8] If we focus only on missions, we neglect our responsibilities. If we focus only on our local efforts, we end up with a debilitating inward focus. We need both.

Only a few will go as missionaries to another nation, which then becomes their "Jerusalem." But everyone must be involved with the world by giving financially and by praying. Never allow commitment to be without cost. The cost of world missions has increased greatly year by year. To keep sending missionaries, Christians in their home country will be called upon to sacrifice greatly, to put "feet" on their commitment to the world. Will we do it? Or will we turn inward to building the evangelical establishment where the Gospel can be heard dozens of times weekly in every city? Without involved Christians committed to world vision, the twentieth-century evangelical church will relegate itself to the backwaters of history.

In each congregation there is no limit to what one committed man or one committed woman can do to influence the whole. How desperately we need the power of men and women unreservedly committed to a vision, a calling, and the world. This power will come from ordinary people, not superstars. They will be people who have recognized that life without a central focus is futile, and that their commitment can make a difference. Their lives will leave a mark, not a blur, on other people and the world.

NOTES
1. Nehemiah 2:18
2. Matthew 28:19-20
3. John 15:16
4. John 4:35,38
5. Isaiah 6:8
6. Isaiah 6:9
7. Acts 26:18
8. Acts 1:8

17
Commitment and Spiritual Maturity

WE ARE TO GROW UP IN ALL ASPECTS
INTO HIM, WHO IS THE HEAD,
EVEN CHRIST.
Ephesians 4:15

A stranger walking down the road would have heard the sound of flesh being scraped, accompanied by a muffled groan. What he saw would have been worse. It was a man sitting on the ground, covered with sores in every stage of some dread affliction. Some were open with pus and others were scabby; some were scraped and bleeding. No part of the man's pock-marked body was spared—the soles of his feet, the palms of his hands, under his arms, on his face. He looked like a beggar, but everyone knew who he really was. He was Job—rich, a leader, respected, wise.

A group of boys ran up on a dare and spat in his face. Men asked in a murmur what great sin he had committed. Women gossiped that they knew. But only Job knew that he had done nothing. His wife had just said the unthinkable: "Do you still hold fast your integrity? Curse God and die!"[1]

That hurt deeply. Job thought back in the spaces between waves of pain. Only weeks ago he had everything. Then his life crumpled around him. His animals were slain. All that he loved was destroyed. All his children were killed in a natural disaster. Finally, he lost his health and now sat helpless. Only his wife was left, and she had emotionally withdrawn her support.

He rehearsed and reviewed every minute of his conscious life to discover some unconfessed sin, or some heinous betrayal of his God, and found none. In an age when calamity and judgment were synonymous, Job somehow knew that was not the true view of God. He felt all the human emotions—fear, anxiety, depression, anger, and despair—and yet he would not give up on God.

Somehow he knew that all these traumas had a purpose. But what was that purpose? Bit by bit he spiritually struggled through this time and haltingly tried to express his thoughts.

When his children died, he said, "Naked I came from my mother's womb, and naked I shall return there. The Lord gave and the Lord has taken away. Blessed be the name of the Lord."[2] Despite the loss of his children, Job did not sin or blame God. Somehow this ancient pilgrim understood that *God is sovereign* and that he must be committed to God's sovereignty.

Then Job's wife tried to get him to curse God. Job replied, "You speak as one of the foolish women speaks. Shall we indeed accept good from God and not accept adversity?"[3] Again Job did not sin with his lips. He was committed to God *regardless of his circumstances*. He was not a prosperity preacher.

In his despair he said, "But it is still my consolation, and I rejoice in unsparing pain, that I have not denied the words of the Holy One."[4] Job was committed to *God's word and promise*. Pain and poverty could not make him deny God.

In his pain he realized, "My days are swifter than a weaver's shuttle, and come to an end without hope. Remember that my life is but breath."[5] Job came to understand the *brevity of life*, a perspective that many never comprehend.

He asked in desperation and humility, after being confronted with possible sin by a so-called friend, "I know that this is so, but how can a man be in the right before God?"[6] He now focused on the central question of how to be just before God, and he found the very way: "I would have to implore the mercy of my judge."[7] He knew, though he still struggled and argued, that God's mercy was his only solution.

As Job later argued his case he said, "Though He slay me, I will hope in Him."[8] That is the final commitment—the ultimate hope in God alone—*faith*. Job even had a glimpse of life after death: "If a man dies, will he live again? All the days of my struggle I will wait, until my change comes."[9] "And as for me, I know that my Redeemer lives, and at the last He will take His stand on the earth. Even after my skin is flayed, yet without my flesh I shall see God; whom I myself shall behold, and whom my eyes shall see and not another."[10] An incredible conclusion for an ancient man who knew nothing of a resurrection. In his pain he grew to know that *he would see God after death.* Would he ever have known it without the suffering?

It seems that Job finally came to a conclusion: "But He knows the way I take; when He has tried me, I shall come forth as gold."[11] The suffering was a trial and would purify him. True, Job was pushing his own innocence, and rightly so. He had "treasured the words of His mouth more than my necessary food."[12] He knew God would justify him even if he died physically.

In his final reflection, Job came to ultimate reality: "Behold, the fear of the Lord, that is wisdom; and to depart from evil is understanding."[13] Now he knew it in a way that exceeded a memorized proverb learned from his father. He knew it through his suffering.

In this remarkable account, Job pleaded his earthly case of good works to no avail. And God confronted him by saying, "Will the faultfinder contend with the Almighty?"[14] In submission, Job said, "Behold, I am insignificant; what can I reply to Thee?"[15] He puts himself at God's mercy and says, "I have heard of Thee by the hearing of the ear; but now my eye sees Thee; therefore I retract, and I repent in dust and ashes."[16]

The lessons of Job are many, but certainly one of the most significant is the way God worked sovereignly with one man to reveal Himself to him and to bring him to *spiritual maturity.* But many suffer and do not grow to spiritual maturity. Instead they become bitter and their spiritual beings wither to impotence. What is the difference? The difference is basic commitments. Job was committed:

> to the sovereignty of God in *every* aspect of his life;
>
> to trust God regardless of circumstances, even in great difficulty;
>
> to God's word and God's promises;
>
> to a view of life that superseded any materialistic focus and that saw life as more than just living for himself;
>
> to the mercy of a loving God;
>
> to a hope based only in faith;
>
> to a hope beyond this life.

To understand, grasp, and practice these truths leads to spiritual maturity. But these truths are not just taught and believed in a classroom or church. They are experienced in the laboratory of real life, often in the context of difficulty and hard times. What takes believers through these hard times? *Commitment.*

Commitment is absolutely essential to spiritual maturity. Spiritual commitments made in the midst of the stress and strain of living and at the turning points of life are the keystones of that maturity.

A byproduct of growth is renewed commitment, or recommitment. So often the same issues reappear and challenge us, and we must remake the same commitment that we thought was permanently made ten or twenty years ago.

In an earlier chapter, I claimed that the Great Commission is to be the central vision for every believer. However, God also places the growth of the believer to spiritual maturity on an equal footing.

It could be said that maturity is an integral part of the Great Commission—intrinsic in the concept of discipleship.

God's great purpose is that we "become conformed to the image of His Son."[17] Paul's purpose for believers was to "present every man complete [mature] in Christ."[18] He said also that God gave gifted people for equipping the believers, "until we all attain to the unity of the faith, and of the knowledge of the Son of God, to a mature man, to the measure of the stature which belongs to the fullness of Christ."[19] Spiritual growth is not an option, but a necessity. And maturity is the goal.

As I reflected on the meaning of maturity, I realized that there is a central mark of maturity. In the human physical realm, maturity is gauged by when a person is able to bear or father children. A tree is mature when it bears fruit. A stalk of grain is mature when it can be harvested. In all creation, fruit-bearing is the preeminent mark of maturity.

Certainly the spiritual realm differs little. A mature believer bears fruit of two kinds. The first is that of character and holiness of life. The second is becoming a spiritual parent either by leading others to Christ or by adopting a baby or growing Christian.

Jesus taught, "I chose you, and appointed you, that you should go and bear fruit, and that your fruit should remain; that whatever you ask of the Father in My name, He may give to you."[20] The entire fifteenth chapter of John intrinsically ties abiding in Christ to fruit-bearing. In fact, from verse 16 we could legitimately join answered prayer to fruit-bearing. Could lack of fruit-bearing, and thus lack of spiritual maturity, significantly hinder answered prayer?

One word summarizes the mark of the spiritually mature man or woman—obedience. Simple obedience extends from the mind and heart and expresses itself through the will. In the midst of the abiding discourse of John 15, Jesus characterizes his true friends: "You are My friends, if you *do* what I command you."[21] He also says, "If you keep My commandments, you will abide in My love; just as I have kept My Father's commandments, and abide in His love."[22] The condition for Christ disclosing Himself to a man or woman is obedience: "He who has My commandments, and keeps them, he it is who loves Me . . . and I will love Him, and will disclose Myself to him."[23] Christlikeness—spiritual maturity—is obedience.

In a society so given over to sexual impurity and marital unfaithfulness, immorality is a serious challenge to a committed maturity. Job, in testing his past life, testified, "I have made a covenant with my eyes; how then could I gaze at a virgin? . . . If my heart has been enticed by a woman, or I have lurked at my neighbor's doorway, . . . that would be a lustful crime."[24] The trap that quickly erases spiritual maturity lies in sexual lust and immorality. The spiritually mature man or woman makes a lasting commitment to holiness of life and sexual purity.

We know that God ultimately blessed Job and increased his wealth and happiness far beyond his previous circumstances. But this was a different Job, one who had suffered and was tested.

One final comment: Growth never ends. We

can never quit. The battle goes on and so do the trials. The body gets old, but the soul becomes rich and youthful in its maturity. And, as Moses was unaware of his shining face, the spiritually mature person rarely is aware of his maturity. He simply lives his commitments.

"And Job died, an old man and full of days"[25] — still committed and maturing spiritually.

NOTES
1. Job 2:9
2. Job 1:21
3. Job 2:10
4. Job 6:10
5. Job 7:6-7
6. Job 9:2
7. Job 9:15
8. Job 13:15
9. Job 14:14
10. Job 19:25-27
11. Job 23:10
12. Job 23:12
13. Job 28:28
14. Job 40:2
15. Job 40:4
16. Job 42:5-6
17. Romans 8:29
18. Colossians 1:28
19. Ephesians 4:13
20. John 15:16
21. John 15:14, italics mine
22. John 15:10
23. John 14:21
24. Job 31:1,9,11
25. Job 42:17

18
Backing Out of Commitments

THEREFORE, MY BELOVED BRETHREN,
BE STEADFAST, IMMOVABLE, ALWAYS
ABOUNDING IN THE WORK OF THE LORD,
KNOWING THAT YOUR TOIL IS NOT
IN VAIN IN THE LORD.
1 Corinthians 15:58

One man. Two incidents from his life. Two commitments with vastly different results. The first brought into being one of the wonders of the ancient world. The second caused the death of thousands of his countrymen.

It was one of those days that every man, woman, and child would talk about the rest of their lives—and pass on to their grandchildren. People danced in the streets. A holy revelry penetrated every street and alley of Jerusalem—the city of David. War had ended. Israel had won. And now the priests carried that small box called the ark of

God with two poles thrust through rings on the sides. David the king led that incredible parade, punctuated every six paces with the sacrifice of an ox and a fatling. There was shouting and blowing of trumpets. As David danced and celebrated like a teenage athlete, he remembered his anger of three months ago when they tried to move the ark on a cart, in a way God did not approve. He remembered his friend Uzzah struck dead by God. David had learned to do things God's way.

After hours of this procession, they brought the ark to its place in the tent of meeting. David generously gave food to all the people and then went home exhausted.

Not long before, he had built a spectacular house for himself. As he sat in the comfort of the king's house he meditated on the Lord, as was his habit. He sang and prayed. Then a thought struck him like an arrow in his chest: "Here I sit in splendor while the ark of God sits in that desert dweller's shelter, a tent." He felt chagrined.

He made a commitment in his heart to build a house for the ark of God. He shared his grand vision with his friend Nathan, who was a prophet of God. Nathan was ecstatic over the idea and as a prophet gave David the go-ahead.

That night God had a short chat with Nathan. He must have reminded him to check in before giving an "answer from God." He instructed Nathan to tell David that he could not build this temple since he was a man of war and blood. But God also made a covenant to bless David, and promised to establish his kingdom. He commended David's heart in his desire.

So the shepherd-singer-soldier king retracted his commitment. Perhaps he "lost face" before his friends, yet he stopped his plans.[1]

Time passes to find an older king, battered by revolt led by his son, shamed by his treachery with Uriah and Bathsheba, and generally exhausted by the responsibilities of ruling. He has another idea—to take a census of all the people. This time his friend Joab tries to tell him that this is a foolish decision contrary to God's will. David probably tells him to obey his orders and get on with the job.

Then he realizes his sin—too late. The result is a pestilence from God claiming the lives of 70,000 men.[2]

In the first case, David responded immediately to change his direction and decision. In the second case, he stubbornly refused to back away from his decision. Both were cases in which decision or commitments were made that needed to be changed.

Overcommitment of time, energy, and effort is a plague of our Christian society. Call for commitments to activities and ministries shower upon every seriously spiritual believer. But no one person can do everything. And as God gives a person new direction and its consequent commitments, something must go—if not other commitments, then a person's health. A key to rational spiritual living is to be able to recognize when a commitment should be terminated or reduced.

Certain commitments are lifelong and must never be terminated or reduced—only deepened. This would include commitment to the lordship of Christ, marriage, and obedience to the Word. Even in these, however, the accompanying activities may change with need.

Other commitments—to certain individual activities, to group activities, and to people—are limited. In this arena there are no unlimited commitments. No one has the right to ask for unlimited commitment to anyone or to anything but God Himself. We change, circumstances change, and so our commitments must also adjust to reflect our deepening understanding of what God has for our lives.

Some commitments are unwise. People may make them impulsively or emotionally or with insufficient information. When a person realizes that a truly unwise commitment was made, it would be even more unwise to continue that commitment.

Do not misunderstand. One should not vacillate and wander in and out of commitments every time circumstances change or the pressure gets too great. Commitments are made to be kept, not dodged. But when a commitment is clearly not of God, we must back out.

In general, our commitments to activities or people should be limited, especially in terms of time. Think of most commitments in six to twelve-month segments, with open options for renewal. Activity and people commitments are almost always an outward expression of deeper, long-term commitments to God. We must not compromise them. The obvious, surface commitments that must grow out of the deeper vows can then alter and change. Periodic reevaluation is not only desirable, but imperative. Do not make commitments lightly, since backing out can be painful and embarrassing.

If you find yourself frequently backing out of obligations and commitments, it probably means that you make them too lightly and do not have basic life commitments against which to measure time commitments. Only on rare occasions should you break your commitments.

Consider Ecclesiastes 5:4-6:

> When you make a vow to God, do not be late in paying it, for He takes no delight in fools. Pay what you vow! It is better that you should not vow than that you should vow and not pay. Do not let your speech cause you to sin and do not say in the presence of the messenger of God that it was a mistake.

God takes our vows seriously. Making a commitment to Him is no light matter. God *will* hold us responsible. These are the deep, lifelong vows and the specific vows of obedience. These we cannot—must not—change. This is reinforced in the discipleship passage of Luke 9:62: "But Jesus said to him, 'No one, after putting his hand to the plow and looking back, is fit for the kingdom of God.'" Our commitment to follow Christ with all our heart, mind, and will must remain firm and deepen.

These passages do not apply to the short-term commitments to activities (number of hours in prayer, meetings, and Bible studies, for example) and people (such as time with friends and supporting others' activities). Yet such commitments need to be made. After all, faithfulness and dependability are hallmarks of Christian character. Let's do what we say. Let's keep our commitments and not shift with every changing circumstance.

Faithfulness in the activities that build on

our lifelong commitments are the only way these deep commitments become reality in life. The accomplishment of a ministry vision must be accompanied by faithful people. Vision without action is of no value. Yet to fulfill one vision means purposely not fulfilling another. We have only so much time and energy.

But what do we do with Psalm 15:4—"He swears to his own hurt, and does not change?" The context of this verse is integrity and a holy life. This person *chooses* to make a commitment that he *knows* will hurt him, such as loaning money at no interest, or taking a loss, or extending himself physically or emotionally to meet another's need. It does not mean that we can never back out of a commitment.

In many matters, a legal contract that binds us is required. Or we make an equivalent verbal contract. In many of these cases we must keep the contract or commitment. But in many cases we can *ask* to be released.

After serving in the Air Force for thirteen and one-half years, I still had one and one-half years remaining. I applied to be released from this commitment, and it was granted. It could just as easily have been denied, in which case I was willing to fulfill it.

An example in Scripture is that of Onesimus, a slave owned by Philemon. Onesimus ran away and was converted in Paul's ministry. Paul sent him back to Philemon, asking that he be released from two significant commitments—his crime in escaping and his slavery. Paul recognized these legal and moral commitments, but he appealed to Philemon's higher commitment to God and to himself.[3]

In some instances, a person may not totally back away from a commitment, but may lessen the time demands related to it. Again, he should not act precipitately.

What conditions should be met before a believer changes a specific commitment? Consider these suggestions:

1. You have prayed and have the clear leading of God.
2. Keeping the commitment would hinder your fulfilling more basic lifelong commitments.
3. Due to time pressures, you must drop some commitment.
4. Backing out of commitments has not been a pattern of your life.
5. You are not escaping a God-ordained pressure or just being easy on yourself.

As you consider your commitments, carefully review these verses: "Many a man proclaims his own loyalty, but who can find a trustworthy man?"[4] "The plans of the diligent lead surely to advantage, but everyone who is hasty comes surely to poverty."[5]

NOTES
1. See 2 Samuel 7
2. See 2 Samuel 24
3. See the book of Philemon
4. Proverbs 20:6
5. Proverbs 21:5

19
Aberrations of Commitment

THERE IS A WAY
WHICH SEEMS RIGHT TO A MAN,
BUT ITS END IS THE WAY OF DEATH.
Proverbs 14:12

From the time of his birth he seemed doomed to a life of tragedy. He was the son of a prostitute — and no one ever let him forget it. His father took him into his family, but he was always an outsider. Growing up as an unwanted son left its mark in his inner being. But Jephthah had one thing going for him: he was a born leader. Seeing this, his brothers drove him out of the family, and he ran off to another country.

Later, the Amorites attacked these Israelites of the family of Gilead. The Israelites had forsaken God and as usual repented when they were about to be wiped out. But they had no leader for the battle, so they sent for Jephthah. He chided them and extracted a promise from them to accept his leadership.

Day after day he worked to negotiate with the Amorites until it became obvious that they would have to fight. Jephthah was afraid. He knew he could not win without God's blessing. He prayed. He wrestled. Then an idea struck him: "I can make a deal with God." He was seemingly unaware that God had already committed Himself to victory for Israel. Jephthah's "deal" was a vow to God—a tragic vow. He said, "If Thou wilt indeed give the sons of Ammon into my hand, then it shall be that whatever comes out of the doors of my house to meet me when I return in peace from the sons of Ammon, it shall be the Lord's, and I will offer it up as a burnt offering."[1] He imagined one of the sheepdogs that always rushed out to meet him, or a cow or sheep that often shared the protection of the house. That should be a good, religious bribe for God.

Jephthah fought and won a great victory. As he returned, no dog or cow or sheep emerged— only his daughter, his only child. She came singing and dancing with tambourines to honor her victorious father. His heart sank. His vow. His only child. What could he do? "I have given my word to the Lord, and I cannot take it back."[2]

And so it was done. The knife. The blood flowing off the altar from her pierced body. The fire and the stench. And Jephthah thought he was honoring God.[3]

God never asked for the vow. He cannot be bribed. God would never have held Jephthah to such a foolish vow. He should have realized his stupidity and sought God in forgiveness and praise for victory, and offered a proper offering of thanksgiving through the priests.

Where were the priests? Where were the wise men? Where were the godly men who would keep their foolish leader in check? Gone. Weak. Ineffective. Deceived by victory to think that this was of God.

Not every vow is right. Not every commitment has God's blessing. Any good thing can be used in an evil way. There is never a scriptural basis for a conditional commitment: "If God does _____. then I will do _____." Such is a perversion of the nature of God. He cannot be bribed. Yet it is so human to think that way.

We may recoil at this tragic story. Yet we can so easily make similar commitments, which God will not bless.

No one can forget the tragedy of Jonestown in Guyana where hundreds of men and women were duped by Jim Jones. They not only made a blind commitment to his authoritarian leadership, but they obeyed the final vow to drink the poison. This was an extreme act, even in the world of cults. But its seeds can be found in many places. Unquestioning subservience to an authoritarian leader or leaders always creates a perversion of commitment.

The Christian must never make an unconditional and unquestioning commitment to any person. And he must never request such a commitment of anyone. Every leader must stand the test of both biblical soundness and a godly life. Any church or group that insists on total loyalty, total commitment only to them, or unquestioning obedience to a set of their rules must come under careful scrutiny. No human authority—a church or paralocal church group—can claim exclusive commitment. I do not mean to imply that meaningful commitments to a body of believers, their vision, and activities cannot be made. The issue is that it cannot be demanded in a total sense. Even churches or groups that have sound doctrine can violate the concept of commitment when they impose or extract unbiblical vows.

A second aberration of commitment is bound up in the term *legalism*. It is so easy to establish a set of good rules and then to obey these rules thinking that such obedience somehow earns us favor with God. The greatest cause of religious bodies wandering from the truth of Christianity is the perversion of the doctrine of grace. It is quite clear that our salvation commitment is of grace: "For by grace you have been saved through faith; and that not of yourselves, it is the gift of God; not as a result of works, that no one should boast."[4] Yet many who fully accept salvation by grace live under the delusion that grace ends there and the ongoing Christian life is lived by works. Others fully agree that the Christian life can be lived only by the grace of God, yet they adopt a set of rules or actions that put them back under bondage. These rules often are meant to aid their walk with God, but they often develop into a means by which believers supposedly earn God's favor.

This trend has happened repeatedly in history— meticulous keeping of a holy day, pilgrimages to a holy place, crawling up steps to a holy altar, or abuse of one's body, all keyed to the concept that such acts will earn favor with God. Do we exhibit some of these tendencies? Lists of prohibitions, rigid attendance standards, compulsive devotional lives, repetitive prayers, and a refusal to associate with non-Christians are all examples of things that, though possibly good in themselves, can lead to a "grace-earning" posture. Thus commitment to do such things in a legalistic way constitutes not only an aberration of commitment, but a serious misconception of grace.

The Pharisees made certain commitments or vows to escape some biblical responsibilities. For example, through a religious vow they avoided supporting their parents. Do we avoid witnessing for fear of developing friendships with sinners? Do we allow commitment to ministry or church activities to keep us from properly leading our family? Such are aberrations of commitment.

Commitment to politics, a social position, or nationalism can also lead not only to an illegitimate commitment but to a misconception of the Christian life and mission. God is not a socialist, a democrat, a communist, a liberal, or a conservative. Nor is He American, British, Indonesian, Kenyan, or any other nationality—not even Jewish in the nationalistic sense. A "religious" commitment to such concepts or entities cannot have biblical sanction. National loyalty and personal convictions are legitimate. But to believe that the Bible teaches an exclusive political system or favors a particular country does violence to biblical truth. So, too, an excessive commitment to a political system or country is an aberration of commitment.

Other commitments, while not illegitimate or unbiblical, can easily replace those deep life-giving commitments that God wants us to make. Some good commitments consume our energy and lives in a debilitating way. I see sincere Christians committing themselves to such things as health foods, home education, culture, cleanliness, orderliness—even one's marriage and family—in such a way that all other commitments take second place. Please do not misunderstand. These good things can be useful— but only if they function in proper perspective.

But how can we know? Very simply, nothing is worthy of our commitment that is not firmly rooted in Scripture. Make your commitments in areas that the Scriptures clearly command, or that clearly support biblical imperatives.

NOTES
1. Judges 11:30-31
2. Judges 11:35
3. I am aware that there are differing interpretations of the story of Jephthah's vow to God. One view, expressed in this chapter, is that he physically sacrificed his daughter. This interpretation is supported by F.F. Bruce in *The New Bible Commentary: Revised,* pages 268-269 (Grand Rapids, Michigan: Wm. B. Eerdmans Publishing Co., 1970). Another view is that Jephthah's daughter spent the rest of her life in celibacy, serving in the tabernacle. See Gleason Archer's *Encyclopedia of Bible Difficulties,* pages 164-165 (Grand Rapids, Michigan: Zondervan Publishing House, 1982) and John W. Haley's *Examination of the Alleged Discrepancies of the Bible,* pages 239-240 (Nashville, Tennessee: Gospel Advocate Company, 1974).
4. Ephesians 2:8-9

20
How to Make Realistic Commitments

AND THE TWELVE ... SAID, "IT IS NOT
DESIRABLE FOR US TO NEGLECT THE
WORD OF GOD IN ORDER TO SERVE
TABLES. BUT SELECT ... SEVEN MEN OF
GOOD REPUTATION, FULL OF THE
SPIRIT AND OF WISDOM, WHOM WE
MAY PUT IN CHARGE OF THIS TASK.
BUT WE WILL DEVOTE OURSELVES TO
PRAYER, AND TO THE MINISTRY
OF THE WORD."
Acts 6:2-4

Tension filled the meeting room. The past weeks had been a leaping from one victory to another for the men who gathered. Thousands had believed in Christ. Even a short prison stay ended in victory. The new believers were forming into a loving, sharing band of co-laborers. Even the grisly incident with Ananias and Sapphira turned into a clear impetus for a life of integrity.[1]

Now one of their inner fears had come to pass. Internal squabbling had begun. Factions formed and sides were taken. The apostles had been confronted soundly with legitimate complaints. The problem was with serving food to the widows they had decided to care for as a shining testimony to the community. The Greek-speaking Jews were critical of the native Jews because their widows were not fed.

Even the apostles grumbled: "With so much to do, why do we have to be bothered with this matter?" "But you are responsible," replied the representative of the Greeks. "You set up the plan—and it's not working."

After considerable discussion, some new thinking emerged. The apostles realized that they were in fact responsible. But did they have to see to it themselves? They studied what Moses had done when he was overcommitted and was rebuked by his father-in-law.

"It doesn't make sense for us to take time from our primary task of preaching God's Word to look after the proper distribution of food. Let's have the people choose seven trusted men to take charge of that task. We must give ourselves to prayer and the ministry of the Word."

Had the apostles taken on this extra commitment, they would have violated their primary commitment to pray and to preach the Gospel. They could have been pressured by the people to do it— or could have felt they would offend people by not tending to it personally. But the Scriptures report, "The statement found approval with the whole congregation."[2]

Overcommitted. Too many activities. Running to and fro. Too busy. All these words describe the frantic, committed Christians of today. No wonder a conscientious believer reading this book might say, "All I need is more commitments to drive me to a nervous breakdown. I've got all I can handle."

That is only too true. But it is also a misunderstanding of the meaning of commitment. It is not a commitment to more activity—though activity can sometimes be involved. The committed Christian should not have to live a frantic lifestyle to demonstrate his devotion.

First, we must recognize a hierarchy of commitments. Second, we must understand that God will never ask for commitments that we cannot fulfill.

Consider a structure of commitments like this:
Lifelong commitments
  —to be
  —to do
Limited-time commitments
  —to do personally
  —to people
  —to activities

Lifelong commitments must be few, and very significant, and deeply rooted in Scripture. These commitments "to be" are issues of mind and heart that result in deep character traits. They would include matters of lordship, holiness of mind, and central life vision. Personally, I am committed to keeping Christ as Lord of my life and to testing everything else by that lifelong commitment. I am driven by a vision for multiplying laborers and disciplemaking—in my home, in my city, and in the world. I am personally committed to pursuing a life of integrity and holiness. It also involves an inner commitment to be faithful to my wife and family.

The lifelong commitments "to do" must only include activities that are essential, and are usually not highly restrictive as to the specifics. For instance, I am committed to a lifelong, daily quiet time, but I have not specified the length of that time daily. I do that year by year.

Some lifelong commitments could be to honor your marriage, to be involved regularly with believers, to carry on a regular study of Scripture, to witness, to keep from immorality, or to be obedient to what you know God wants you to do. It may include your faithfulness on your job. These lifelong commitments are not necessarily time consumers, but should form the very fiber of your life—the way you think and live. How they are translated into specific activities fit more under limited-time commitments.

Most of our time and energy is consumed by our limited-time commitments. Yet they are necessary to put practical meaning into the deep lifelong commitments. These nonpermanent commitments should rarely extend more than six to twelve months. At that point we can choose to extend them, but we are not obligated to do so.

The limited-time commitment "to do personally" involves such important things as length of quiet time, time in prayer, Scripture memory, physical exercise, and many other items that we personally choose to do. Some might be for pure enjoyment or recreation, some for family or home needs, and some to support our spiritual life.

Limited-time commitments "to people" and "to activities" overlap in many ways. They include commitments to Bible studies, prayer groups, conferences, planning committees, boards, community activities, church or para-local church demands, hobbies, sports, and a myriad other demands on one's time. We must update these in light of our priorities and personal or family needs.

Most of the commitments in this book relate to lifelong commitments of heart and mind, activated by specific acts of the will. How do they interact? As an example, I may have a lifelong commitment to Bible study, but would only set goals or make commitments to a group on a six to twelve-month basis.

Most people are reluctant to add a regular weekly or biweekly activity on an open-ended basis. They need a termination point to evaluate effectiveness and their own need or contribution. On the other hand, a commitment to a one-time activity such as a conference is much easier to make since it is an event. But even these events pile up and need evaluation in light of our personal need and vision or calling. One problem is that many people do not have lifelong commitments to vision and calling against which to evaluate the short-term commitments. Most make such decisions impulsively, depending on how they feel or how much time they have.

Now comes the crucial question. How does one practically make significant commitments—particularly lifelong commitments? I have found four predominant settings in which deep commitments tend to be made:

1. Conferences of more than one day
2. In the process of in-depth Bible study
3. In the midst of personal crises
4. Through small groups or person-to-person discipling

Note the absence of church services or single

meetings. They often are too short to focus on deep commitment. Certainly decisions are made in such meetings, but they generally result from the third setting—a personal crisis.

Many Christians have a hit-and-miss relationship with God. They grab a few minutes for a quiet time, rush into a worship service, skim through a book—but never give extended time to God. I believe that every Christian needs to give a few days a year to God, preferably in a conference setting, where they are challenged and also have time to reflect on their personal spiritual needs. Over two to six days, we surrender our minds to Jesus as Lord and His Word in a way we cannot do at any other time. I have repeatedly seen people make life-changing lordship commitments at such times. I would also suggest that this *not* be a family conference, or your attention will be given mostly to children rather than your own spiritual needs.

As a person commits himself to several hours a week of Bible study, God will certainly open up key areas of his life—particularly if the study is applied to life, not just to knowledge. God uses His Word to speak to the deep needs of our lives. It is "living and active and sharper than any two-edged sword, and piercing as far as the division of soul and spirit, of both joints and marrow, and able to judge the thoughts and intentions of the heart."[3] Give His Word a chance to work.

Personal crises—depression, marriage struggles, children's problems, job issues, tragedy, and illness—bring us face-to-face with reality and spiritual need. Sometimes God needs to place us in a kind of "Job" experience to get our attention.

When this occurs, some people make significant spiritual decisions—and others harden their hearts.[4]

Some make emotional decisions and do not know how to activate the new commitment in their lives. My strongest recommendation when you make a commitment in the midst of a personal crisis is to share it with a mature Christian who can help you develop practical steps to ensure that you go beyond the mind and heart to the will. Make yourself vulnerable and accountable.

The final setting is that of small groups or person-to-person discipling. Where you have regular accountability to people, hopefully in the context of Bible study, you are stimulated to fulfill the commitments you have made as well as to make new ones. The environment of fellowship and accountability provides a fertile ground for lasting spiritual decisions.

The Scriptures describe only two means of expressing commitment: written and verbal.

Nehemiah, whose life vision and calling were discussed earlier, led the people to make a written commitment, or covenant. As they finished building the walls of Jerusalem, Ezra read the law and the people confessed their sin and reflected publicly on how God had dealt with them. Nehemiah 9:38 reads, "Now because of all this we are making an agreement in writing; and on the sealed document are the names of our leaders, our Levites and our priests." Chapter 10 then lists them by name.

Joshua challenged the people of Israel to choose whether or not they would follow God. They replied and made a verbal commitment: "We will serve the Lord our God and we will obey His voice."[5] Thus

Joshua wrote the words down as a witness. As an immature youth, Jacob made a very conditional verbal vow to God, even though God made an unconditional covenant with him.[6] It was not till years later that Jacob wrestled with God and made a deep commitment that left him lame for life.[7] These, and many other pledges recorded in Scripture, were verbal commitments made to God publicly or in prayer.

When you make a commitment to God, write out briefly what that commitment is. Then sign and date it. This not only records the covenant in writing, but it also clarifies to you the specifics of your commitment. You may use the form in the appendix for this.

As you make these commitments, I suggest that you assure them by two actions. First, jot the date and a key word of reminder in the margin of your Bible by a verse that expresses the commitment. Second, share the commitment with a fellow believer for accountability. Secret commitments are rarely kept. Don't be afraid to express your personal commitment to the Lord and to others.

Your commitments should relate directly to Scripture. Therefore, as God leads you to specific commitments, attach them to a Scripture verse or passage. The passage need not be the one that led you to the commitment, but should relate to it or express it.

For instance, if you make a commitment in the area of holiness of life or sexual morality, you might use 1 Thessalonians 4:3: "For this is the will of God, your sanctification; that is, that you abstain from sexual immorality." 1 Peter 1:16 would also relate to this area. If your commitment involves trimming your schedule and adjusting your priorities to your vision, you could use Philippians 3:13-14. If your commitment is to be under someone's authority, you could use Hebrews 13:7 or 17. If your commitment is to be steadfast in hard times, refer to Hebrews 12:11 or James 1:2-4.

When you tie your commitments to Scripture, the Lord can use the passage to remind you and allow the Holy Spirit to deepen those commitments. I suggest that you then commit the verse or verses to memory. The verses that attach to your lifelong commitments should be written in your notebook, calendar, or planning diary—some place where you will see them frequently.

Finally, make your shorter-term activity commitments realistic and reasonable. Two hours a day in prayer, ten hours a week in Bible study, or four group meetings per week may be commendable, but unrealistic for any length of time. Better to make more reasonable, attainable goals and exceed them than to set a pattern of burdensome commitments.

NOTES
1. See Acts 5:1-11
2. Acts 6:5
3. Hebrews 4:12
4. See Hebrews 3:7-11
5. Joshua 24:24
6. See Genesis 28:13-21
7. See Genesis 32:22-28

21
Enemies of
Commitment

BE ON THE ALERT. YOUR ADVERSARY,
THE DEVIL, PROWLS ABOUT LIKE A
ROARING LION, SEEKING SOMEONE TO
DEVOUR. BUT RESIST HIM,
FIRM IN YOUR FAITH.
1 Peter 5:8-9

From the beginning it seemed that he made wrong choices. He traveled to a new land with his uncle. Generously, his uncle, Abraham, gave him the choice of living anywhere he wished. Lot had been looking over the country and already was plotting where the best land was located. He looked at a valley that was "well-watered everywhere"—a rarity in this desert-like country. The valley was like a garden.

The major cities in the valley were called Sodom and Gomorrah.

His choice was fatal. The Bible records, "Now

the men of Sodom were wicked exceedingly and sinners against the Lord."[1] But Lot still went there. He was deeply influenced by that decadent society, even though he apparently did not participate in the homosexual immorality.

God decided to destroy Sodom, but sent two angels to rescue Lot and his family. His daughters were engaged to men of the city who mocked him when he tried to get them to leave. Even Lot didn't quite believe the angels—or simply didn't want to leave. "But he hesitated. So the men [angels] seized his hand and the hand of his wife and the hands of his daughters . . . and they brought him out."[2] Lot was told to "escape for your life." But his heart was still tied to the city of sin, and he talked them into allowing him to go to the small neighboring town.

Sodom and Gomorrah were destroyed and remain desolate to this day. To complete his infamous choices, Lot's daughters got him drunk, had sexual relations with him, and bore children of that incest.

We hear no more of Lot. His commitments were his downfall. Materialism, greed, sexual sin, a decadent environment—and finally incest—kept Lot from godly commitments and ruined his life.

Satan has prepared many enemies of commitment to God—both subtle and blatant. Though several of these have been mentioned earlier, a summary may help us see the enemy more clearly.

Sexual immorality and *sexual lust* of the mind destroy and prevent godliness and godly commitment. David's sin with Bathsheba multiplied itself a thousand times in his son Solomon. David repented. Solomon indulged. How many godly men and women who have begun to make deep commitments have been sidetracked by lust and immorality? The Christian community is riddled with the results as they desperately try to put their lives together again. Lot saw the danger and ignored it. And his life ended in shame.

Materialism intrudes with such attractive alternatives to a godly life. Lot was led by a lust for material things. Materialism and a focus on things, money, worldly possessions, and comfort keep us from significant spiritual commitments.

Busyness without clear vision and purpose takes our eyes off what really counts. We become so intent on a frantic pace of doing, that we bypass the real issues of life in Christ. Even good Christian busyness can sidetrack us from true commitment.

Fear always lurks in our hearts as we step out on faith in our commitments. We fear the consequences of total commitment in spite of God's promises of blessing. Fear controlled Jonah as he ran from God. The events of the next days of his life consumed him with terror as he lived through the storm and the days in the belly of the fish. Then, even in reluctant obedience he could not fully commit himself to God's plan and cause.[3]

Coldness in one's spiritual life greatly squelches the fires of commitment. But worse yet, coldness creeps in so subtly that the person hardly perceives what is happening. What is coldness? Lack of desire for God. Lack of desire for God's Word. Lack of desire for obeying God. Lack of desire for serving God. That lack of desire puts a chill in our love for Jesus Christ and we become spiritually insensitive—paralyzed in keeping previous commitments and prevented from making others. And we continue in coldness—the walking dead of the Christian community.

Laziness keeps many from making or keeping deep spiritual commitments. The wise man of Proverbs aptly observed, "How long will you lie down, O sluggard? When will you arise from your sleep? 'A little sleep, a little slumber, a little folding of the hands to rest'—and your poverty will come in like a vagabond, and your need like an armed man."[4] Physical and spiritual laziness leads to spiritual poverty and an invasion of sin that robs the believer of spiritual vitality. The sad part is that most Christian laziness expresses itself by filling the time with selfish occupations such as excessive television, hobbies, or sports. Satan will do anything to keep believers from making deep commitments.

Wrong peer influence deeply affects how we think and act in our Christian lives. "He who walks with wise men will be wise, but the companion of fools will suffer harm."[5] Exclusive association with believers who are carnal or who display little spiritual vitality in their lives will do nothing but drag us to their low level of spiritual commitment.

Find men and women who challenge your spiritual walk and thinking, and whose lives radiate a love for Christ. "Iron sharpens iron, so one man sharpens another."[6] If you want your life to be characterized by significant commitments, don't allow half-hearted Christians to somehow convince you that lukewarmness is acceptable. The message of God to the Laodiceans pierces our hearts with fear and determination to pursue a fervent walk with Christ: "I know your deeds, that you are neither cold nor hot; I would that you were cold or hot. So because you are lukewarm, and neither hot nor cold, I will spit you out of My mouth."[7]

An enemy is someone who sets out to do you serious harm. These enemies of commitment are as dangerous as a person who attempts to take your life. Each of them will tempt all Christians and can keep them from the life-changing steps of spiritual commitment. Enemies like this must be destroyed, not played with or tolerated. Given any quarter, they will consume you. Meet these enemies directly with the force of decision and the power of discipline, daily feeding in the Scriptures, and the empowering of the Holy Spirit.

NOTES
1. Genesis 13:13
2. Genesis 19:16
3. See the book of Jonah
4. Proverbs 6:9-11
5. Proverbs 13:20
6. Proverbs 27:17
7. Revelation 3:15-16

22
A Step Beyond

COMMIT YOUR WORKS TO THE LORD,
AND YOUR PLANS
WILL BE ESTABLISHED.
Proverbs 16:3

Listen to a parable.

A man had just been released from prison. The years of incarceration had taken their toll. He was haggard, hungry for love, and in desperate need of physical food. He had been bound by chains and lived in semi-darkness for so many years that freedom was almost unbelievable. But now he was free—totally. A new regime had come to power, a regime of kindness and truth.

He was led stumbling to a room where he was washed, his bleeding wrists and ankles were treated with great care, and he was given new clothes. It was too much to believe. His mind could hardly absorb what was happening.

To this point, everything had been done for him. He was led, guided, and gently ministered to. But now he desperately needed food, and he stammered out his request. There were murmurs of approval. The guards smiled and told him a great meal was prepared. They helped him to his feet and led him to a door. A guard opened it and stood aside, motioning for the prisoner to go in. He froze in fear. His bloodshot eyes widened. All he could see was his cell and the chains. He screamed. The guards grabbed his arms as he tried to run. They had seen this happen before. They looked through the door and saw a banquet table laden with food. They told him what they saw, but that they could not, and would not, force him to go in. But his eyes saw only the prison cell. How could they have done all this for him and then led him back to that dreaded cell?

Long discussion ensued as the prisoner calmed down. He finally agreed to go in. He approached the door—and stopped. He still saw the cell. He simply could not make his feet move. He now believed his rescuers, but seemed paralyzed with indecision. What he saw and what he was told was in that room were radically different. Would he believe what he saw and felt?

Finally he realized that he must trust his rescuers. He falteringly stepped across the threshold. Suddenly the prison cell vanished, and he found himself staring at a table filled with food. Fear left and a deep peace descended on his mind and body.

A voice said simply, "Welcome. You made the

right choice. But I had to allow you to choose, for only then will you know you are truly free. Welcome to the full freedom of your new life."

Reading this book may have taught you about commitment—but nothing happens without a step of decision. All the knowledge you may have will never change your life unless it is accompanied by decisions of commitment.

In our parable, the promise was clear that one step would lead the man to food. But his mind could not grasp or comprehend the blessing of this "step of commitment." His mind was blinded by fear, his past, his mistrust of his rescuers, and his reluctance to take a risk. He desperately needed the food for his growth and healing. Yet he *would never know* until he made the step. There was no force-feeding.

Commitment is never vicarious. Only a person's own commitment allows him to reap the blessings. That commitment requires a step of faith.

Choose. Decide. Step across. Step out. Knowing must be accompanied by obedience. Desire must be accompanied by doing. And usually this commitment is very simple. The only difficult part is to take the step.

Where is God dealing with you now? In your mind? In your heart? In your will? God desires to capture all three. Tozer said that "no part of man will do. God wants all."

Satan will mount a great battle to keep you from making significant commitments. Fear. Doubt.

Selfishness. These enemies and many others will attack as you begin to take that step. And even after the commitment, Satan will do all he can to cast doubt and to nullify the step of faith. But a real step of faith in commitment can never be nullified. God will sustain you.

The great choices of your life can begin now. Life offers no greater reward than the deep fulfillment of a life of commitment.

Appendix

A written statement can help finalize your commitment. This was the pattern of Nehemiah:

Now because of all this
We are making an agreement in writing;
And on the sealed document
are the names of our leaders,
our Levites and our priests."
Nehemiah 9:38

The following can profitably be used to express your commitment in writing. Each of us needs the extra urging and accountability that such a device can provide. Make copies of it to use for several areas of commitment in your life.

PERSONAL COMMITMENT

Lifelong _____ Limited-time _____

Key Scripture: _____

How God led me: _____

_____

_____

_____

_____

My specific commitment: _____

_____

_____

_____

_____

Date: _____ Signed: _____

Commitment shared with _____

on _____